Bassin' in New England

Bassin' in New England

A PRACTICAL GUIDE
TO PRODUCTIVE BLACK BASS ANGLING
IN THE SIX STATE REGION

by William Chauvin
and Carl Apperson
Photographs by Mike Carroll

THORNDIKE PRESS • THORNDIKE, MAINE

ACKNOWLEDGMENTS

To the Fish and Game Departments of the New England
States, the bass clubs, conservationists, and dedicated
fishermen who have generously offered their assistance in
the gathering of the material used in this book — many
thanks.
A special thank you to Bert's Sport and Tackle of
Pepperell for their help with the equipment photographs.
And most of all, a very special thank you to our wives.
Without their support and understanding throughout this
project we might never have seen its fruition.

Library of Congress Cataloging in Publication Data:

Chauvin, William, 1949-
Bassin' in New England.

1. Bass fishing—New England. I. Apperson, Carl,
1944-   . II. Carroll, Mike, 1946-   . III. Title.
SH681.C43 1985   799.1'758   85-2800
ISBN 0-89621-089-8

Design concept by Joanna Young.
Book design and layout by Lynn Ascrizzi.
Cover design by Jonathan Graves.
Special thanks to Tom Chamberlain.

To clear air, clean water, and good fishing, and the people who enjoy them.

PUBLISHER'S NOTE:

Rules and regulations governing both open-water and winter bass fishing vary greatly from state to state and from year to year. Please check with the individual state's fish and game department for current information on season dates, license fees, bag limits, and regulations governing specific waters. A list of these state agencies is located in the Appendix.

CONTENTS

INTRODUCTION

The sound of a fancy high-powered bass boat racing past me was enough, I was sure, to scare all the fish right out of Hickory Hills, where I was trying to fish on a late afternoon in May. The sun was on its way down, and long shadows fell over the western edges of the lake's contour.

I shook my head in dismay as I waited for the yawing and pitching of my small flat-bottomed wooden boat to settle down from the wake caused by the monster that had just passed.

"They must be in a frenzy trying to find a lunker before the sun sets," I said to myself.

Minutes later, I ran across the boat and the two guys in it as they trolled some huge deep-runners alongside a causeway on the shaded side of the lake. I eased in close to a great big pine, the boughs of which hung way over the water, not fifty feet away from them.

"I thought you said there was great bass fishing at this lake," I heard the bigger of the two say to his friend.

"Ah, shut up and fish!"

"If I come home empty-handed again, my wife is sure to get on my tail about this expensive rig and all this gear I bought. I can't stand hearing that again!" he explained as he cast his lure way out behind the boat.

I chuckled as they trolled out of eavesdropping range. Then I rigged up a Rebel surface lure, and chucked it real easy under those pine branches.

"There ain't no bass in this 'ere lake!" I heard the big man shout as they trolled their way back. "Nobody will make me believe that there is!" he exclaimed, just as one huge tug on my line brought me to attention. A big 'ole lunker just rose up out of the shade and was slapping itself silly all over the water next to those pine boughs, trying to shake my lure.

"Look at that!" The man's friend yelled as I struggled to keep this mossyback on the line.

"Must be seven or eight pounds!" I heard one of them yell as I got that big bass in the net. I held it up by its gill rake to admire.

Just then, that frustrated man in his fancy bass boat cracked his expensive rod over his knee and threw it in the drink with a mighty splash. I just grinned as I turned my boat around and headed for home with my evening's supper.

"There ain't no bass in this 'ere lake!" I cannot count the times I have heard that — even at tournaments here in the Northeast, from the lips of bass professionals who come from all over the country to finish off a tour in New England. Some become discouraged after a morning of fishing and leave before afternoon, when old bigmouth begins his feeding frenzy.

This defeatist attitude has led many fishermen to discount one of the truly exciting challenges to be found anywhere in the world of freshwater fishing — the black bass of the Northeast.

I was born in Fredericksburg, Virginia, and have fished many southern states, including Virginia, Maryland, North Carolina, Florida, Louisiana, and Alabama. Since 1963, when I moved north to Massachusetts, I have fished all over New England and New York State. After 18 years of fishing the Northeast and competing in bass tournaments here, I have discovered what I call "a whole new ballgame" when it comes to fishing for bass in New England.

I had to learn all over again. Down south, the waters are, for the most part, murky and muddy. Up here, the waters are clear — you have to be sneaky when hunting bass in the Northeast. The bass are more leery and seem to have keener senses; vibrations travel better in the clear New England waters than in the murky southern ones. I find the bass don't get quite as large, but they give you a better run, and they FIGHT — oh, how they fight! They get right out of the water and dance. I find Northeastern bass fishing, on the whole, most challenging.

Carl Apperson

I was introduced to the pleasure of bass fishing by Carl some time ago, after years of stalking only trout. Born and bred in New England meant that the only fishing worth the time and energy was trout fishing. That notion has been a hard one to let go, but now, having succumbed to the "mystique of the bass," I am truly grateful for my introduction to a whole different sport, one that is as unique and as challenging as stalking the native favorite, and gaining in popularity all over the Northeast.

From the wide and wooly expanses of the Quabbin Reservoir in western Massachusetts, where the bass grow wild and wary, to one of the thousands of small quiet ponds that dot the countryside of Maine, where the sublime and secret beauty of the wilderness enthralls even the most traveled of fishermen, New England offers variety and challenge unequaled in any other region of the United States.

Carl Apperson and I decided to write a book on this long-neglected subject, offering it as a guide to those who wish to explore the nearly unlimited potential New England has as a bass fisherman's paradise. We hope to prove that good bass fishing can be found not only in the southern and far western states, but here in New England as well.

If you are a Northeasterner, an avid bass man, or a novice fisherman looking for some advice on the subject, come along with us and take a look at bass in general and the northeastern bass in particular. It is our hope that we can give the reader a good working knowledge of how, where, and when to hunt the black bass in New England.

William Chauvin

Bassin' in New England

CHAPTER **1**

KNOW YOUR FOE

What makes a bass a bass — the difference between smallmouth and largemouth bass — what makes the New England black bass such a unique challenge.

If you are an experienced bass angler, you already know that to hook up with a bass, you must first think like a bass. Know your foe! Know his likes and dislikes, his favored environments, what makes him comfortable, what makes him uncomfortable, and what entices him to strike. Familiarizing yourself with every aspect of the lifecycle and habits of the black bass, and the special idiosyncrasies of the bass of New England cannot be over emphasized. This is particularly important if you desire to hunt bass successfully time after time and under a myriad of conditions.

Because the bass of New England are not native to this area (having been introduced gradually since the late 1800s), they have adapted to an environment foreign to them. During this adaptation process, New England black bass have acquired some unique survival tactics. Learning what makes a bass a bass, particularly these New England bass, should be your first consideration.

Largemouth and smallmouth bass differ in their habits and preferences. A good working knowledge of the differences between largemouth and smallmouth bass will be helpful in acquiring your limit on any given day.

There is much controversy among bassmen as to which species, the largemouth or the smallmouth, is the better fighter. You will find that the majority of bassmen believe that the largemouth is the more challenging of the two. These anglers will expend their energies exclusively in pursuit of the "bucketmouth." This does a great disservice to the smallmouth bass, and to the bassman! The smallmouth, because he differs in range and habitat and is much more suited to the cooler waters of New England, has established himself in principal fisheries all across the six-state region. Both species pose challenges and because their habits differ, the two offer bassmen a well-rounded experience, as the plan of attack must change as the quarry changes.

New England offers great scenery along with great fishing.

Identification

Smallmouth and largemouth bass are collectively known in New England as black bass, although they are not literally black and are not really bass at all, but rather the largest members of the sunfish family — *Centrarchidae.* One of the easiest ways to identify the two fish is, as their names suggest, to inspect the size of the mouth. The maxillary bone of the upper jaw of the largemouth extends to beyond the eye; the upper jawbone of the small-mouth does not.

Another way to differentiate between the two is to check the dorsal fins. The dorsals of both fishes are really two parts connected by a membrane. In the largemouth, this membrane is so narrow that the two sections of the fin seem to be separate fins; in the smallmouth, the separation is not so noticeable.

Identification of these fish by their color can sometimes be difficult. The color and markings differ a great deal depending upon the type of environment they inhabit. The smallmouth is usually a bronze, brassy color, but factors such as water clarity, food supply, and the amount of sun will change the shade of this fish significantly; in some of the more northern ponds and lakes, he can appear to be nearly as green as the largemouth.

The largemouth is dark green (almost black) on its back, fading to a greenish yellow on the sides. Smallmouths usually have dark vertical bars along their sides; the largemouth's markings appear as a dark horizontal band from its head to its tail.

When the smallmouth is still very young, it can be easily identified by its tri-colored tail. From its body outward, the tail is colored in stripes from orange to black to white. Both fish have deep husky bodies — and a propensity for using this hulk to put up an admirable fight when hooked!

Distribution

The black bass, though indigenous to North America, is not native to New England. The smallmouth originally ranged from the St. Lawrence River and the Great Lakes region to the Mississippi and Ohio River areas, while the largemouth originally extended from southwestern Canada through the Great Lakes to Mexico and Florida and up the Atlantic coast as far north as Maryland.

Both the largemouth and the smallmouth were introduced into New England in the late 1800s. They now extend as far west as Hawaii; they are enjoyed by fishermen in England, France, and Germany, and are becoming well-established in South Africa. In Canada, one or the other or both can be caught from Nova Scotia to British Columbia.

All of the New England states enjoy thriving populations of both fish. Continued efforts by government agencies, with the cooperation of bass clubs and their members, to monitor the management of these sport fish will insure the continued success of black bass fisheries.

Carl shows off a fine example of the New England largemouth.

Size and Growth Rates

All fishermen, particularly bassmen, have stories to tell about that "once-in-a-lifetime lunker" they landed. There are some of those lunkers around New England, to be sure. To give you an idea just how skillful the bass is at thwarting his foremost predator — man — let's look at the average lifespan of this fish.

Most bass live from seven to nine years (*if* they successfully elude the fisherman's hook); but some fish live to be 16 years old! The growth rate of bass varies a great deal, depending on the water temperature, the amount and type of food available, and the amount of competition for food existing in the same body of water. It was found in studies done in New Hampshire, for instance, that the yellow perch is a natural competitor of the small-mouth bass for food. Bass and perch populations will fluctuate with the amount of food available, thus keeping each population within certain limits.

A lake that is overpopulated with bass may have a stunted population — the majority of the bass will be underweight and undersized. The growth rate also slows, even ceases, at temperatures much below 50 degrees; it is easy to see why bass in New England grow at a slower rate than bass in southern states.

The average black bass harvested in Maine is 14.2 inches long and weighs one and one-half pounds. The overall average size of the bass taken in northern lakes is one and one-half to three pounds for the smallmouth and between two and four pounds for the largemouth.

These figures are averages, though, and there certainly are lunkers out there. The new state record for largemouth in Vermont was set in 1982 by James Sproat of Poughkeepsie, New York when he landed an 8-pound 4-ounce lunker at Lake Hortonia. An 11-pound 10-ounce largemouth, taken out of Moose Pond in 1968, is the record for Maine; in 1970, Thompson Lake in Maine gave up an 8-pound smallmouth.

These northern lakes produce some nice specimens in spite of the cooler waters, and if you would like to go further north to prove that some good fish grow there, the Canadian record smallmouth taken out of Macauley Lake, Ontario weighed 9 pounds 2 ounces.

Feeding

Bass thrive in the heat of the south, but they also adapt quite readily to cold northern winters. When winter food is meager, bass may resort to "mudding the bottom." They know that by sifting through the mud they will benefit from the nutrients contained in it.

There is much discussion about this theory. Many believe that bass stop feeding completely in wintertime, going into a state of semi-hibernation. This is a reasonable explanation of why bass are seldom caught through the ice. The truth is that bass *can* be caught through the ice; we will discuss some of these techniques in Chapter 6. We have seen, when cleaning our catch after ice fishing, bass with stomachs full of mud, which goes to support our beliefs.

In warmer weather, bass will lunge completely out of the water after food. This is common knowledge to fly fishermen who have seen bass jump a fly before it even hit the water. Douglas Hannon of Odessa, Florida, a renowned bass expert, notes that "bass have the eyesight and capability of trapping food in the air. They must be observant to find this food, and they can easily see the manmade dinner as it sails above the surface toward their lair. They will chase it, strike it, and make a mistake that thrills the bass purists intent upon outsmarting this great game fish."

Bass are carnivorous, and their diet consists mainly of acquatic and terrestrial insects, crayfish and other types of crustaceans, snails, worms, leeches, small fish (several different species), frogs, tadpoles, mice, and moles. They have been known to down a baby duck now and then.

A bass has the ability to eat almost anything that will fit in its mouth; thus, it adapts readily to different environments and different food supplies.

Spawning

The male bass is extremely aggressive in protecting his nest during spawning season, which makes him susceptible to the angler during this period. This is the reason for restrictions on bass fishing during the months of May and June in New England. (See individual state chapters for more information.)

In late spring when the water temperature has reached approximately 60 degrees, the male bass uses its tail to fan out all the debris over a bottom area about 30 inches in diameter. The smallmouth arranges small gravel around the edges of the depression it has created, and builds up layers of stones in the middle. The largemouth prefers to spawn in shallow weedy areas, but the preparation of the nest is similar. The female lays her eggs a few at a time as the male fertilizes them. At this point, the eggs stick to the nesting area.

The female soon leaves, and the male takes over protecting the nest, fanning the eggs to keep them clean of silt, fungus, and minute predators. The same female, or another, may come back later to deposit more eggs in the same nest. At this time the male bass is most vulnerable to the fisherman. He will viciously attack other fish or any type of intruder, including such things as jellyworms, poppers and the like.

Smallmouth eggs hatch in three to five days at warm temperatures, and in a week to 10 days in colder water; the largemouth eggs take a bit longer.

The tiny fry, each surrounded by a yolk sac, remain in the nest until the yolk is absorbed, which takes from six to 15 days. Then the fry become free-swimming, and the male ceases to protect the nest.

The young fry school as they feed on plankton and grow rapidly, to fingerling size by autumn. As they grow older, they tend to separate, each going its own way.

Male bass mature at three to six years of age, females somewhat later. The male usually has less average length than the female at maturity.

Favored Environment

In New England, water temperatures can range from cold to very warm in a single lake or pond, and can change very rapidly. Bass move from one hole to another, at another water level, when the conditions become uncomfortable.

Bass are always seeking two things: the most comfortable place in a particular body of water, and the area where food is most immediately available. *"I'm hungry."* That is the dominant thought of a bass.

The largemouth bass prefers warmer, slow-moving rivers such as the Nashua in north central Massachusetts, and shallow, weedy, muddy-bottomed lakes, such as Dickerson's Reservoir in Lunenburg, Massachusetts. They thrive in waters that have an average summer temperature of around 70 degrees.

Smallmouth prefer clear, cool waters and are found in faster-moving streams and in the gravelly, rocky sections of lakes such as the larger New Hampshire waters.

In New England, you will frequently find both the largemouth and the smallmouth in the same body of water. New England rivers provide some areas of backwater that offer plenty of weedy cover that meets the preferences of the largemouth, and some rocky, gravelly, faster-moving areas that are more favorable to the smallmouth. Our lakes and impoundments also offer the variety that will attract both fish.

Both the largemouth and the smallmouth are shallow water fish. They will hole up in the deeper shaded-water areas during the heat of the day, then move into the shallower areas at dusk and stay there until dawn.

Just as the New Englander has to adjust to the extreme conditions of weather, so does the bass. We have all the conditions of the four seasons: the cool dampness of spring, the blistering humid summers, the dry cool falls, and the cold winters. The feeding habits and movements of bass are dictated by water temperature, food supply, and the oxygen content of the water (see Chapter 4).

Now that you have become somewhat familiar with the lifestyle of the bass, read on and learn how to apply this knowledge successfully as you stalk bass throughout New England.

Smallmouth territory, Lake Champlain.

CHAPTER 2

EQUIPMENT

Preparation — rod, reel, and line — tackle, live and artificial baits — boats and motors — the best choices for New England waters.

Imagine it is 4:15 a.m. on a spring day in June. You can hear a lonely meadowlark's song, and the distant answers of its cousins. There is just that whispered hint of daylight as the sun squints through the feathery clouds, creating a yellow haze along the horizon. The damp morning air causes you to yawn the sleep out of your lungs, and you are wide awake. The pensive stillness is broken only by the sound of your boots as you cross the beach to the bass boat which rests at the foot of the shoreline.

There is not a ripple on the water. The whole lake shines like a freshly polished mirror, reflecting the morning light through the mist. You are going out with us to hunt the bass. Anticipation is high, though not a word has been spoken.

We place our gear in the boat and shove off into the misty waters of a central New England pond. The streams of fog dance perpendicular to the warm water. They move aside as we approach, scattering into the deeper fog — swallowing us up into the mist as we move out.

The yellow dawn has started to light the lake in iridescent splendor. We spot the V-shaped wakes of one- and two-pounders, racing just below the surface in search of the morning minnows and the early flies.

Carl tells us he saw tadpoles just about ready to lose their tails a few days ago.

A pair of Canada geese stretch out their long necks and honk at us as they pass overhead. The hum of the motor breaks the silence, and we are off to a cove covered with lily pads, straight across the lake. The bass are finished spawning and are waiting, hungry for their prey; we are ready to oblige, with tackle boxes full of jelly worms and other goodies.

Keep his head up and use a large long-handled net to boat your bass.

There was an eight-pound hawg taken up in the far end of this cove just yesterday, so we'll try that area first. The smell of bass is everywhere, hanging on the moist air; as we approach the shallows, the scent becomes more pronounced. . . the bass are here, all right!

The thrill felt on a perfect fishing morning like this will wake a bass man out of a sound sleep. He knows the signs that mean good fishing, and should be prepared to hunt such a superior foe as the black bass.

Now is the time to start thinking about equipment. Do you have the right gear for fishing New England waters? No matter how many trips you make to your favorite New England lake or river, each will be different. New England is unique in its diversity of landscape, climate, and rapid shifts in the weather. For this reason, you can never prepare too much for the New England bass! Your approach to bass fishing here will be different than your approach to bass fishing in other regions of the country; of course, there are similarities, too.

Clothing is something well worth thinking a bit about before starting out. When it comes to bass fishing, particularly in New England, having the right clothing can make the difference between enjoying yourself and suffering for hours until you are on shore again.

In your plans, include comfortable clothing for the *whole* trip. It is easier to remove excess clothing than to freeze when the weather changes, or when you underestimate the temperature. It may be 55 degrees on shore, but once you are out on the water, the air temperature will likely be much lower. After about 20 minutes — when frost begins to form on the gunwales! — you will be anything but comfortable without that jacket you left on shore.

A T-shirt, followed by a flannel shirt or sweater and a jacket, will give you layers of clothing you will be able to peel off as the weather gets warmer; a hat for shade from the sun, with a visor to help diminish glare, is also invaluable.

Once your fishing wardrobe is in shape, prime consideration is the type of rod and reel you will use. The rod and reel should be an extension of your arm, and should work smoothly and accurately in as close to an effortless movement as possible. Remember, you will be casting several hundred times in a day, and fatigue sets in fast when using a bulky or out-of-balance rod and reel. A considerable amount of attention must be given to your choice of rig — to the balance between your rod, your reel, and yourself. Achieving this balance needn't be expensive, if you take into consideration some of the important basics explained here.

Rods

In New England, two types of rods are most often used. One is the short (5½-foot) model for the fast action and short casting of our rivers. These "river rods" are great for getting lures into tight areas and under brush accurately without getting caught up in the structure.

The second type of rod is the 6- to 6½-foot rod, which will extend your reach to the fullest and give that added distance and accuracy necessary in long casting. When selecting either of these rods, keep these three things in mind:

1. Backbone — the rod's ability to set the hook and keep tension on the line at all times without breaking.

2. Sensitivity — the tip of the rod is like an antenna — it transfers all the information about what is happening at the end of the line down the rod to your hands. With the proper sensitivity, you can feel the difference between large and small fish, tell which direction the fish is running (side-to-side or up-and-down), and whether you are running a lure across rocks, weeds, or over drop-offs.

3. Weight — the less the rod weighs without sacrificing backbone, the less casting fatigue.

Most name brand rods come in light, medium, and heavy actions. Medium action will enable you to use a wider range of lures of different weights, all of which you will need to bass fish in New England. The medium-stiff rod will also compensate for minor timing errors, offering positive hook-setting ability.

Graphite rods outperform the old metal, fiberglass, and cane rods in backbone, sensitivity, and weight; most graphite rods weigh less than eight ounces. Graphite has been our personal preference for years, but feel free to explore some of the new technology.

Boron rods now on the market claim to offer 25 percent more strength than fiberglass or graphite and a unique design that allows vibration to travel 100 percent faster through the rod. A tungsten filament of .004" diameter is woven into the rod to provide strength and sensitivity.

Ceramic eyelets offer little resistance to the line and wear very little. Metal eyelets wear easily and become grooved, threatening damage to the line and creating drag. Ceramic's super-hard molecular structure is so dense that the line slides over it as if it were greased.

The best type of handle depends on the type of reel you decide to buy. For baitcasting, a pistol grip handle is preferred. For an open-faced spinning reel, an extended straight handle is the way to go.

Rod handles come in plastic and foam rubber, cork, and teakwood. Let your personal preference be your guide here; no appreciable difference exists except for a slight difference in weight. We have used all types of handles and tend toward the comfortable and lightweight plastic and foam rubber models.

The Reel

The second half of a well-balanced outfit is the reel. Our favorite, the open-faced spinning reel, is the all-around best bet for bass fishing in New England waters. Its life expectancy is high; open-faces are designed to wear very little, giving you your money's worth. There are very few backlashes with the quick bail-release system of an open-faced reel — ideal for the run of a super bass. The spinning reel also offers positive hook-setting ability, and this is important if you intend to boat your fish.

Hooks are made with very sharp points, but a bass's jaw is hard and slippery, and you need to sink the hook as deep as possible. To set the hook well you will need to bring the rod up hard and fast and then, at the top of the set, hold the rod and take up the slack. The open-faced reel offers a good amount of the control needed without the bulk and weight of some of the baitcasting rigs, which are unnecessary in New England waters where the bass caught rarely weigh more than ten pounds.

The open-faced spinning reel is mounted suspended below the rod handle, offering better balance. The spool is open — when a cast is made, the line flows freely off the stationary spool, offering added distance and accuracy, especially when the line is guided with your thumb and forefinger. The open-faced reel also handles a wide range of bait. By changing the line size and sometimes even the rod to a lighter or heavier action, baits from a fraction of an ounce to several ounces can be used.

Another strong reason that the open-faced spinning reel is your best bet is because it is probably the best reel to use when casting into the wind. More distance and accuracy can be achieved with an open-faced spinning reel under windy conditions.

Baitcasting

There has been a considerable difference of opinion among bass fishermen concerning the best type of outfit for bass fishing. Some professionals believe that baitcasting is the only method worth utilizing when bass fishing. This may be true in tournaments, particularly in the south, where monster bass are sought — and caught — but is less true for the average New England angler.

Baitcasting (or levelwind) reels are made up of a line carriage that layers the line on a revolving spool. They are accurate, offer easier handling of heavier lines and lures, and offer the ability to horse in weightier catches fast.

But baitcasting requires a sensitive thumb action to stay in control of the line to deliver the lure to the pre-selected spot. The baitcasting outfit is difficult for the beginner.

Light tackle is nearly impossible to use on a baitcasting rig, and backlash is a common problem for the beginner. Backlash (or bird's nest) is caused when the line loosens on the reel and catches on itself while the spool keeps turning, causing many yards of line to snarl and knot together. The cause of backlash may be bad eyelets, frayed line, the use of too light a lure for the line and reel, etc. But more often, the cause of backlash in baitcasting is improper use of thumb pressure.

Closed-faced Reels

Closed-faced spincasting reels are preferred by young and old alike because of their single action, push-button design. Closed-faced reels are easy to operate, but have a nasty tendency to tangle and fray the line. This is often caused by a worn pick-up pin, rough edges on the cone face, or a badly worn felt guard. All can be corrected by replacing the worn parts.

The biggest trouble in a closed-faced system is caused by small grains of sand that collect inside the cone, around the spool, on the line, and along the felt guard ring. It is important to keep these clean and well-oiled.

Closed-faced spincasting reels are the most popular reels on the market today because they are simple to operate and relatively trouble-free. They can cast a wide range of lure weights, and are also good to use when casting into the wind. A closed-faced reel limits the accuracy and distance attainable, although some of the more expensive models are reasonably effective.

Balance

The reel you select should complement the rod used to provide the maximum efficiency and comfort. This is the critical "balance" between the rig, the rod, the reel, and yourself. To check for this balance, put the rod and reel together, then slide your finger up from the reel set to one inch off the upper grip. If the rod rests on your finger without tilting, it has an excellent balance.

To balance a baitcasting reel with a pistol grip rod, you may have to try several different combinations of rods and reels. Generally, baitcasting rods are from five to six feet long. Find the rod that conforms to your hand and feels smooth in its action. Flex your wrist and practice casting if possible. The rod and reel that work best together will be the combination that is comfortable and least fatiguing.

A well-balanced rig means comfort and ease of operation.

The third leg of the outfit is probably the *most* important — the line. Remember, there is only a thin piece of monofilament between you and old mossy-back.

Many fishermen use the same test (strength) line for all of their fishing. This can cause a lot of heartaches when you are saying a fast goodbye to your lure, 40 feet of line, and a great big lunker after the line has snapped under the pressure.

Bass line for use in New England should be from 10- to 14-pound test with little memory (some line, when wrapped on a spool, "remembers" the curve of the spool and will curl as it sits on the water).

Most lines on the market are reliable as to their test, but they do not stay around long enough for you to find out because of the way most fishermen treat them. Here are some tips on keeping your line as fresh as possible:

Change the line on your reel twice a year. Cut the first 15 feet of line off every third or fourth time you make a trip to your favorite spot. Mono has a tendency to fray from such things as the fish's sharp teeth or a dead lily pad ruffing up the edge.

Heat can cause line to lose strength. On the reel or in your tackle box, a temperature of 150 degrees Fahrenheit can cause line strength to be cut in half or more. Small checks and cracks can also form along the length of the heated line. You would be wise not to store your tackle in the car trunk for long periods of time.

You will want a line with little memory and a lot of natural clarity. Paying a little more and buying any one of the top name brands will be well worth it when that once-in-a-lifetime lunker is dancing on the end of your line!

The Bass Boat

What differentiates a bass boat from other craft? You can catch bass from any kind of craft, but what makes the perfect bass boat for hunting the black bass in New England? Some of the questions you should ask yourself when looking for a craft designed for bass fishing are:

1. Will I be loading and unloading this boat by myself, from a cartop or trailer?
2. What size lakes and rivers will I frequent?
3. How many people do I fish with usually?
4. In what kind of weather do I usually fish?
5. What are the major comforts I require when I fish?
6. And most important, how much can I afford to spend?

As New England has many small and medium-sized lakes, and many river systems worth fishing (some with limited access), a small to medium-sized boat or canoe is a must if you want to explore our more remote areas. They also can be drifted into mere inches of water, and are favorites for fishing weedier, swampy areas.

But New England also has huge expanses of water that are prone to heavy weather, such as Quabbin Reservoir in Massachusetts, Lake Champlain in Vermont, and Sebago Lake in Maine, etc. A lot of these larger waters require use of a larger and more stable boat with motor. In these cases, a 14- to 16-foot craft is a must to navigate the lakes safely.

Many native New England bass fishermen have a nice-sized bass boat and motor, equipped with a trolling motor, live well, depth sounders, graphs, etc., and also keep a lightweight canoe on hand for those nice quiet little spots they will visit. Let's compare some of the types of crafts available.

First, the canoe — a birch bark, wood-ribbed structure is well out of the price range of the average fisherman, but this is the ideal craft for small lakes and quiet rivers. It is relatively light, strong, and quiet. Its natural color blends well with the surroundings and the water, but it has the tendency to tip if you forget where you are and what you're doing.

The aluminum canoe is good, but noisy! It is strong and can withstand a lot more punishment from the angler and the elements, and has a flatter bottom and is less likely to tip.

The ultimate bass canoe is made of fiberglass, ABS, or other similar material. It is strong, durable, and of medium weight. It glides easily through the water, is quiet, and virtually indestructible.

Unless you plan to anchor your boat in one lake, stay away from the wooden flat-bottoms. They tend to be very heavy and require a lot of upkeep, but are stable and attractive.

The most popular boats are the 14- to 16-foot V-hull and flat-bottomed aluminums. They have all the characteristics of the wooden boats, except they are a lot lighter. They require little maintenance, and they are durable — and some models are even small enough for cartops.

Fiberglass V-hull and flat-bottoms are super-sturdy, last a lifetime and, although they are heavier than aluminum, most of the new ones are unsinkable. They are very quiet and require little maintenance.

The above-mentioned craft are all adequate bass craft. But, now, let's take a look at a craft fully-rigged for bass fishing.

The craft built solely for the purpose of bass fishing has a trolling motor for quiet and slow maneuverability in shallow weedy spots. The floor is elevated and carpeted for safe fishing while standing in the craft. Two swivel chairs, one fore and one aft, rotate a full 360 degrees and raise and lower for your individual comfort. Just behind the bow is a livewell with an aeration unit for keeping your catch fresh and alive. The boat has centrally located controls for your outboard, steering, throttle, and starter, an electronic depth gauge and fish finder, and maybe even a CB rig. Usually, these bass boats also have storage compartments for rods and reels, tackle, dry clothing, and emergency equipment. The outboard is usually from 25 to 50 horsepower, with an automatic trim-tilt.

The trailer built to carry this rig can be backed right into the water. You can just drive the boat right up on it, lock her in, and drive away.

This kind of craft is the bass fisherman's dream!

This basic equipment — rod, reel, line, lures, bait, boat, and clothing — will be all you will need to bass fish New England. As a matter of fact, there are many lakes with facilities for boat rentals right on their shores, so the lack of a boat need not stop you from trying out the treat of a lifetime — bassing in New England.

The Tackle Box

Do not start out by buying that worm-proof box that is chock full of different fancy and colorful lures. The box and maybe one or two of the lures may well end up being all that is of any use to you. Select an empty tackle box that is lightweight, and not so bulky as to encumber you when getting in and out of a boat, or while picking your way through bushes on your way to your favorite offshore spot. It does not matter how large or small your collection of lures is, as long as it contains the ones you know old mossy-back will hit under certain conditions.

Opening Carl's tackle box, we see a plentiful supply of jellyworms of all colors and sizes, from two inch twisters to 9 inch jelly kings. He has a good supply of hooks in sizes ranging from 2/0 to 4/0. Most of his hooks are weedless and some of them are self-weighted. He also carries swivels and slide-weights of sizes from 1/8 ounce to 3/4 ounce.

On the other side of the box are spinner baits — his favorites for use in New England waters are yellow with small blades, yellow and black with small or large blades, and black with large blades. He also has an assortment of Rebel™ lures ranging in size from 3 inches to 5 inches in length, blue with a white underside. We must not overlook the Hula Poppers™, Jitterbugs™, and Heddon's Crazy Crawlers™ that he uses for night noise baits. All these artificial lures are in his tackle box because they are tried and true bass enticers.

There is also room for rubber eels, frogs, and crayfish artificials, which all have their place; we discuss these in more detail in Chapter 4 on technique.

Live or Natural Bait?

You can sure open a can of worms here! You see, all creatures that live around, in, and even above the water are a potential meal for old bigmouth. If it fits in that mouth, that huge tunnel that comprises 30 percent of his body, he will swallow it. With all respect to other gamefish, a bass is the largest and the hungriest of them all!

You can catch bass with shiners, worms, nightcrawlers, grasshoppers, pine bugs, white grubs, flies, frogs, tadpoles, salamanders, wasp larvae, and even horseflies. These are the most basic and easiest to obtain, either by gathering them yourself or by purchasing them at a bait shop.

The term "shiners" refers to tiny fish of many species, but bullhead, chub, and milldace are the best for action and long life on the end of the hook.

Worms have been used through the centuries, world-wide, for all varieties of gamefish. Presented properly, a worm looks to a bass like a three pound T-bone looks to us.

Flying prey such as grasshoppers, horseflies, and June bugs send vibrations over the surface of the water when tossed out there in the late afternoon.

White grubs are abundant in and around garden areas. You see all too many of them when hoeing around those tomatoes and cukes.

Wasp larvae are just a tad dangerous to obtain. Nests can often be found in the eaves of barns, haylofts, sheds, and other old buildings. Keep an eye on the nests as the adults build them. Just before the eggs hatch, exterminate the adults, remove the nests, then remove the larvae one at a time.

The Number One live bait for bass is a frog or a tadpole — both are found in most freshwater areas. These little creatures make up a great deal of old mossy-back's diet. Bullfrogs, tree frogs, leopard frogs — all are fused in the memory of that small brain of a bass. We do not need to wonder what the thoughts of a bass are at the sight of a little green and white frog. "Did someone say, 'dinner is served'?"

CHAPTER 3

SAFETY

How to make every fishing trip safe, pleasant, and productive.

In order to fully enjoy your fishing trip in New England, pay attention to some basic safety rules. As Carl says, "You can't bass fish when you're all 'stove-up' on the front room couch." By following a few basic safety rules, you and your fishing partners can derive maximum entertainment and enjoyment on all of your fishing trips.

You have probably heard this all before but it's worth repeating. When you are fishing in remote undeveloped lakes in the northern reaches of New England or on a 2,000-acre lake in Massachusetts or New Hampshire, nothing should be left to chance.

We always carry a first aid kit in the boat. You need not spend a lot of money for a good, complete kit. A simple kit can be placed in a plastic bag, tied with a bread tie, and placed in a coffee can closed by a plastic lid to render it waterproof. The following items should be included:

1) One-inch gauze rolled bandage
2) Four-inch gauze pads
3) Rubber bands (they make excellent finger tourniquets)
4) Roll of one-inch adhesive tape
5) A small plastic bag containing cotton balls soaked in alcohol.
6) Chlorinating pills for water
7) Smelling salts
8) Tongue depressors (can be used for finger splints)
9) Sharp, clean knife
10) Wire cutters
11) Anti-diarrheal medication
12) Salt tablets
13) Aspirin
14) Bandaids

We also believe that everyone should have a basic knowledge of first aid. The American Red Cross gives first aid courses in your area — the small fee covers the cost of textbooks, which you keep at the end of the course. For

31

The Nashua River — an environmental success story.

the few hours it takes to complete this course, an invaluable amount of lifesaving knowledge can be yours. It is well worth looking into — contact the American Red Cross in your area.

Perhaps the single misfortune which besets nearly every fisherman at least once in his fishing career is accidentally hooking himself — or a friend. To avoid the possibility of hooking someone or being hooked by someone else in the first place, just follow a little simple courtesy when fishing with a partner. Map out the angles of casting that each will use. This pre-determined imaginary boundary can prevent many an unhappy incident.

Another common cause of accidental hooking is backlash or improper casting. One-finger casting always presents a danger when the finger that holds the line slips during the backstroke of the cast and the line is released in back of you. Always remember to cast in a line that does not cross your partner's space. This will avoid catching him with the hook meant for old bigmouth.

Boating safety is another area where taking a few precautions and following a few simple rules can prevent a lot of unnecessary grief.

The most common causes of boating accidents are:

1. Overloading. Follow the boat manufacturer's maximum weight limit — it's marked somewhere on the craft. Have you ever seen four people try to fit into a two-man canoe? We have watched this comedy of errors many times; under these conditions, someone is bound to end up in the drink.

2. Alcohol. Some people think that the perfect place to hold a drinking party is in a boat. Just like driving a car, drinking and boating **do not mix.**

3. Excessive Speed. Excessive speed, particularly on an unfamiliar lake or river, is just asking for trouble. Remember, as the water level rises after a rain, those stumps, rocks, and weeds that were visible yesterday may be fully submerged today. Losing control of a boat at full throttle is no joy ride.

4. Improper Fueling Technique. Never light a cigarette, or have any open flame, near the area where you are filling a gas tank.

5. Improper Loading and Unloading. Carl remembers one afternoon that began pleasantly in fishing the shore of a local lake. As he and his partner were casting along the edge of the lake, they noticed a man drive up to the boat ramp and proceed to put his boat into the water. A few minutes went by and they didn't hear the noise of the outboard starting. Carl turned back to take a look and there was the man foundering in the water, gasping, the boat sinking to the bottom underneath him. He had forgotten and shoved off before checking the boat's drain plug. When the boat began to sink, the man panicked. Carl and his friend saved the man and spent the rest of the afternoon drying off.

Maine's Sebago Lake is a good bet for bass, trout, and salmon.

Always make a check list and follow it, step by step, when preparing your boat for launching.

6. Not Observing Weather Conditions. Listen to a local weather forecast before leaving home. You may only be planning on being out there a couple of hours, but weather changes fast in New England, especially in lakes in and around the mountain areas of New Hampshire and Vermont. Lakes in the White Mountains in New Hampshire are particularly vulnerable to nasty, sudden storms.

If you see a storm front approaching when you are out on the water, do not count on being able to outrun it. Head for shore. There are some pretty powerful waves generated by a severe storm, even on New England's smaller lakes. There is also the danger of lightning striking, or of a downpour filling your boat with water, adding weight to the craft and drastically reducing maneuverability.

7. Not Observing Regulations. Be aware of any special regulations on the lake or reservoir you are fishing. For instance, lakes often have areas reserved for swimmers. Observing warning signs along rivers and lakes, or checking conditions on any body of water, can save a spill over a falls or a hairy ride over some white water.

We strongly recommend taking a boating safety course; they're offered by the Coast Guard. Information on classes can be obtained by contacting the nearest Coast Guard office.

Above all, common sense and courtesy can go a long way toward making your hunting trips for old "mossy-back" more enjoyable and satisfying for yourself and others.

CHAPTER 4

TECHNIQUE

Varying technique for lakes and ponds, rivers,
and coastal waters — weather and its effect on
technique — developing your own bassing technique —
boat and shore fishing.

New England is unique in that a drive of several hours from a central
point in the region will take you to no less than seven different types of
fishing waters in six different states. From its cold mountain
lakes and streams to its large reservoirs, wide slow-moving rivers, and
warm coastal lakes and ponds, New England holds every nuance of bass
fishing conditions in its rugged and beautiful countryside.

Needless to say, learning and applying different techniques will be necessary in order to catch the black bass, one of the most clever predators in
the animal kingdom.

What can you do on a lake of 1000 or more acres to simplify the task of
finding old mossy-back and his cousin, the bronzeback?

The first thing to look for is the food supply. Look for supplies of bait
fish, shiners, crayfish, flies, and even small snakes. If you find some of
these in areas of the lake, you can be sure that you will also find bass.

Secondly, locate the flats, weed beds, drop-offs, and ledges. A topographical map of the lake will help simplify this task. Look for structure —
overhanging brush, stumps, logs, rocks, islands — even docks, bridges,
and other manmade structure — in short, any likely hiding place that bass
could use.

Next, check the water temperatures and the depths of the areas you have
chosen. Talk to local fishermen, and check out local tackle and bait shops.
Find out what lures have been popular that season and what areas have
been producing well.

Any information you can obtain before launching your boat will eliminate much of the guesswork involved when fishing an unfamiliar body of
water. The better prepared you are, the more time you can spend actually
catching bass.

A good cast can find bass right from shore.

Although we have used many different techniques successfully, we start in the spring, as a rule, with slow-moving baits — spinners, worms, and deep runners. As the season progresses, we move into the weed beds and flats. As the temperature rises during the summer and early fall, we hunt the bass in the drop-offs and ledges. In the late fall as the water cools off large bass strike with more authority. Perhaps they know that winter isn't far off.

Large lakes and impoundments do a very strange thing during the early spring and late fall. With the aid of the wind and rain, the waters of the lakes turn over, enriching the oxygen content at all depths. This increases the comfortable and habitable range of the bass, and also increases their feeding range, allowing them access to a varied diet. For this reason we leave no bait untried during early spring and late fall.

Small lakes and ponds are probably more neglected than any other waters. Small water acreage does not mean that bass have not been able to adapt to this more confined environment. Some anglers believe that the bass is very territorial and will live out his life in less than an acre of water unless forced by unfavorable conditions to roam farther from home.

Small lakes and ponds are generally much warmer than large impoundments; the temperature may reach 75 degrees even at the bottom of shallower ponds. There may be no structural layering of water temperatures or oxygen content, and bass, in this case, may be active most of the time. In some small New England ponds, bass may be very small or stunted because of lack of room and a limited food supply; but this usually occurs in *very* small ponds. To a child or to the beginner, a pond like this could be an excellent proving ground for future fishing for larger bass.

The rivers of New England offer a challenging experience for the bass fisherman. Most of these rivers are breathtakingly beautiful, and teeming with varied native and migratory wildlife. As we have stated before, the bass makes his home where the temperature and the oxygen content of the water are conducive to his comfort, and the flow of the water in a river causes a natural turnover of water which is constantly replenishing the oxygen supply and maintaining a nearly constant temperature.

Bass in a large river of 15 feet deep or more tend to move more quickly and strike harder at their prey. Spinner baits and four- to six-inch rubber worms are great for this kind of angling. Crayfish are an excellent live bait for use in rivers, because they make up a large percentage of the natural food supply of bass in these waters. Bass are frequently caught on fast-moving rivers after the ice has moved onto some lakes and ponds.

Fishing a river is not, by any means, an easy task; you will work hard for a good string of bass. But the rivers of New England can, and do, produce large fish. It is common to see six- and seven-pounders taken from the Connecticut, and the Nashua River in north central Massachusetts is burgeoning with four- to five-pounders.

The character of a river changes from day to day. The movement of water shifts mud, sandbars, and any structures such as logs, tree limbs, stumps, and even rocks. This has the effect of changing the feeding habits and haunts of bass.

Most rivers in the Northeast have some weed cover along the banks and many shallow backwaters. For example, the Squannacook River in Townsend, Massachusetts, when fished with a four-inch jellyworm jumped across the weeds and dropped into the little pools along the riverbanks, offers some exciting bassing. This technique will excite largemouth to strike every time.

New England offers no end of possibilities for the bass fisherman. One can never get bored with the "same old routine" of fishing here — bass fishing in New England is never routine!

Weather

The weather is the bass's wristwatch. Seasonal changes, and changes in weather patterns, greatly affect when and where the bass will strike. On a sunny day, the shady side of the lake or river, or any sort of overhang that creates a shady spot, will be his favored lair. On windy days, the larger bass can be found facing the wind, which drives their food right toward them.

Springtime brings the bass up from the depths as the spring overturn, a mixing of the water created by the actions of the wind and rain so prevalent in spring, enriches the oxygen content of the water and breaks up the winter layers of temperature stratification. The growth of young leafy plants in shallow water also produces more and more oxygen. Bass increase their activity and start to feed on fry and anything else available in preparation for the spawning season. As they become satiated, and the females are ready to drop their eggs, the summer stratification slowly begins to set in. Gradual warming causes the water to set up in layers of varying temperatures, from the warmest layer at the top to the coolest at the bottom. Usually summer stratification accompanies the hatching of the bass eggs. The bass move into the 65- to 70-degree water and feed savagely for the next two to three weeks.

In the late summer and the early fall, bass become harder to find as the layering of water of different temperatures increases. This is due to the fact that the bass are seeking their ideal environment, where the temperature and oxygen content are most conducive to their comfort.

In late fall, the lakes overturn again and the oxygen supply is replenished. This supply of oxygen will keep the bass alive throughout the winter, as the surface freezes over and the wind no longer has an effect on the water. In the winter, the slow change of the water temperature sets the stage for the whole cycle to be repeated.

Wind strength can also influence the habits of bass on a day-to-day basis. The temperatures of the layers may change as much as two to three degrees per layer, due to the mixing caused on a windy day. Sunlight will also have an effect on water temperature by warming the water gradually from the top.

One good way to eliminate some of the guesswork when it comes to temperature is to use a thermometer and a depth gauge. There are many electronic devices available for this purpose. Most modern bass boats come equipped with an electronic depth gauge, a graph, and a digital thermometer. A press of a button can tell you the depth of the water under your boat, the surface temperature of the water, and can give you a picture of what the underwater terrain looks like, including the location of the fish in the area. Of course, this is an expensive proposition. Adequate results can be obtained by the use of a sounder, a heavy weight that attaches to the hook on the end of your line. By dropping the sounder in the area you intend to fish, an estimation of the depth can be obtained. At this point, a temperature reading can be taken with an ordinary mercury thermometer — let it set at the pre-selected depth for a few minutes, then reel it in as quickly as possible to be read. Repeating the reading at various depths will give you a good idea of the layering of the water in the area. Normally, bass like 65- to 70-degree water, but if the oxygen content of the water is better at a different temperature, they are more apt to be found there.

Fish the spot at the different depths with lures for the surface, medium runners, and deep runners. If you find that you are catching bass at a certain depth more frequently, make a note of the depth and the temperature. It is a sure bet that on that particular day on that particular lake, you will find bass in other areas of the lake at the same depth, and that the oxygen content there must be at a comfortable level for bass.

There are oxygen meters on the market — but they are generally priced above the range of the average fisherman.

Look, also, for creek beds along the bottom of a lake, where a current runs through the lake. There will be a good supply of oxygen in this type of area, where the water is constantly mixing. The temperature is also more constant along the flows of these old creek beds.

Another phenomenon that occurs in many New England lakes is the cold spring — it creates cold spots in the water, and is largely responsible for the addition of minerals, nitrates, etc. to provide nutrition for microscopic life in the lake. The 39- to 42-degree temperature of spring water being introduced into a lake from the bottom is invaluable on hot summer or cold winter days. Bass can often be found lurking just off the cold spots where the temperature may be more constant.

There are some lakes that have no inlets or outlets to create these flows of fresh water that tend to mix the oxygen. These bottled lakes, as they are called, if not turned over sufficiently in the spring and fall, may have little oxygen supply for the winter; when this is depleted, the lake can be the site of what is called "winter kill". Many of the fish in the lake will die because they simply cannot breathe.

Bass are also affected by changes in barometric pressure that occur every day. As a low pressure front moves in, bass tend to slow down, or even stop, feeding. If the low is accompanied by high winds, you may as well pack up and go home.

The best time to be out fishing is when a low pressure system is moving out, just after the pressure starts to rise. Bass feel this change in pressure and respond by becoming more active.

Just before a storm, when the pressure is dropping, you can see fry head into weed cover. We believe that fish just do not like the sudden change in the water temperature brought about when a cold rain hits the surface. The top layer of water may cool off eight to twenty degrees in a flash. It is very similar to when you are taking a nice warm shower and somebody draws hot water in the kitchen. "Yaaah! — That's cold!" It's a shocker and not very pleasant.

Bass can also feel a building high pressure system. As a high pressure builds, bass feed as if it were their last meal. After a high pressure peak period, it is downhill as far as fishing is concerned. But when it is windy on a high pressure system, bass are in a feeding frenzy!

In short, bass will be found where it is most comfortable to be as long as the food supply is good. Look for water that is cooler on a hot day and water that is warmer on a cold day. Look for sites that are well-endowed with oxygen, natural flows of water, springs, etc. Watch the daily forecasts to see the progressions of highs and lows and weather fronts. If you follow these basic rules of thumb, you will soon come to learn for yourself the fine points involved.

Casting

The proper way to learn bass fishing is: as early as possible! There is so much to learn and assimilate that the earlier in life you start, the better trained you will be. But no matter when you decide to learn, remember that experience and observation are your best teachers. What we will do in this section is give you some of the basics — then you must get out there and watch others and by all means experiment on your own. "Practice makes perfect" is certainly an adage that is applicable to bass fishing.

Now that we have you all rigged with gear and boat, and have given you some information on the habits of the bass, let's concentrate on individual technique, which will vary with each lure and location. By far the most important skill to develop and practice is casting. You will want to place that lure or bait in the exact spot you have selected as a probable hiding place for old mossy-back.

Baitcasting reels are best when a fast retrieve could mean the difference between first and second place in a tournament. You will find that a great number of professionals prefer this method for this reason, and that they are often in pursuit of bass of over 10 pounds! The method is hard to perfect, especially for the beginner, and is not necessary for the fisherman who intends to make New England his fishing headquarters.

Spincasting is the preferred method for this part of the country. It offers positive hook-setting capability and an ease of casting that can be developed by even the most inexperienced, while still offering the accuracy demanded by all professionals.

Use your wrist to get the full effect of the rod and reel as they work together. A snap at the point of release could mean the difference between hitting your target and falling short.

Tuning up your cast is a simple matter of practice. Practice at home with any new equipment. Your front lawn is the ideal place to set up a practice target. Take an old tire, cardboard box, or anything that will make a reasonable two-foot-square target, and set it about 15 feet away from where you will be casting. Practice casting with a weight tied to the end of your line until you can hit the target consistently. Repeat this practice with weights which simulate the range of lure weights you will be using. Move the target back to 20 feet, then to 25 feet, etc., until you have developed your casting accuracy for long distances as well as short.

Now get a kitchen chair and repeat the process from a seated position. Many people forget that most of their casting will be done from a boat while seated. You will also want to practice casting from the right and left side and "lopping" the cast out, a sidearm technique useful when having to get that lure under overhanging trees and bushes. By practicing this method you will develop a good judgment of distances and an accurate spot-casting ability.

Some people use a one-handed spincasting technique, using their index finger to control the release. Carl's two-handed release method is one that many of his friends have adopted for the ease of execution and added control it offers.

Hold the rod in your right hand and the line in your left as you cast, using the fingers of your left hand to control the cast by putting more or less tension on the line. This can prove to be quite an advantage in distance as well as spot casting.

A closed-faced spinning reel — just about the easiest to use, with good distance, too.

The open-faced reel offers more control, greater distance.

The baitcasting reel is a favorite of many bassmen, but can be more difficult to master than a spincasting rig.

Closed-faced spinning reels are just coming into their own as far as quality and ease of handling are concerned. This type of reel *requires* a one-hand operation.

Just push and hold down the button and cast, releasing the button at the one o'clock position on the forward motion of the cast. This type of casting is the simplest for the youngster to learn, but is somewhat restricted for the development of additional technique.

The Knot

Now that you have practiced casting and have developed sufficient confidence in your ability, you must put the lure on the end of the line — this requires the right knot. Try to use a knot that will set well. There are many different knots shown in handbooks — almost as many as there are fishermen! It will be trial and error until you find the knot that is right for you.

Carl prefers the hangman's slip knot with a twisted double loop. This knot tends to keep the pressure off the critical point where the line takes the most pressure when setting the hook. The various steps used in the tying of this knot are shown in the following illustrations.

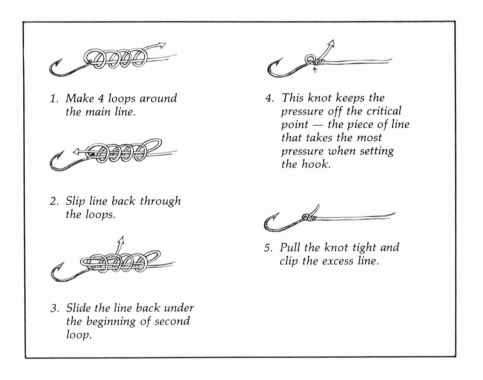

1. Make 4 loops around the main line.

2. Slip line back through the loops.

3. Slide the line back under the beginning of second loop.

4. This knot keeps the pressure off the critical point — the piece of line that takes the most pressure when setting the hook.

5. Pull the knot tight and clip the excess line.

Tie a swivel on the end of your line. Some pros do not use swivels because there is a feeling that the less extraneous tackle showing above the lure, the better the bass will bite. But we feel that swivels help reduce the possibility of line twist and allow for quick lure changing. They come in assorted sizes — the best bet is to match the swivel to the size hook you intend to use. Common sizes we use are 5 and 7.

A few words about some of the different types of lures on the market are included here. There is nothing as confusing as walking into a bait shop and trying to decide which of the hundreds of lures to try. We have already explained the *types* of lures that should be included in your tackle box. Now, let's take a look at them and some of their applications.

The "Rubber" Baits

Rubber worms, or "jellyworms" as they are sometimes called, come in many shapes and sizes. The most common rigs used for the rubber worm are the Texas rig, the weedless rig, and the lead head rig. You can buy these types of rigs complete at most bait shops, but it is far cheaper to buy the worms and hooks in larger quantities and rig them yourself. Jellyworms from four to nine inches long, some with long twister tails, in colors of black, purple, green, blue, or any of the new natural colors, will be invaluable in your bass fishing adventures.

Changing colors of the worms you use can cause bass to strike in different situations. Most recently, on many New England lakes, the blue jellyworm with a long twister tail seems to work well. But you may find, on a given day, that bass are striking green or black worms, so a change of color can often make a big difference.

There are many approaches to casting rubber worms. You will want to cast the worm to an arcing type of landing. You may want to drop the worm in an arc onto some lily pads, flipping it off the pads into open water to simulate a small snake falling off the weeds into the bass's trap. You will also want to jig the worm and bounce it off drop-offs and ledges.

When fishing deeper water, you can use a rubber worm by itself, letting it sink gently and slowly to the bottom, or you can use a weighted weedless hook or a nose sinker to get it down there fast. There are several styles of nose sinkers available. Among those that are preferred and easy to use are the slip-nose slides, the weighted hooks, and the bullet slide.

In the category of rubber baits, hundreds of live bait imitations have hit the market; all can be effective in different situations. Rubber crayfish, eels, frogs, and other baits are all useful to the bass fisherman. When selecting these lures, look for the most lifelike lures — they will give the best action on retrieve in the water.

Topwater Baits

Excellent topwater baits are the Crazy Crawler™, the Hula Popper™, the Jitterbug™, and the Hell Razer™. All these baits float on the surface and simulate the actions of live bait. The Hula Popper™ should be a three-inch size and have a frog color. They work great from June to October in the early morning and late in the day, especially in the shallows. The Jitterbug™ should also be a three-inch size and of a black or frog color — these are most effective at night, and best used in summer.

When using noise baits like these, you will want to flop the lure in and race it to make as much noise as possible. You will want to vary the retrieve from a hard, fast movement to a slow, jerky motion. The more noise you can create, the more vibrations the bass will be able to pick up. The types of vibrations you want him to feel have to be as natural as possible. A bass only eats things it thinks are living and moving.

Spinner and Buzz Baits

For spinner and buzz baits, the Bushwacker™, the Rooster Tail™, and the Bass Hogs™ are excellent. Spinners should be single bladed and half-ounce or less. Yellow-black, yellow-green, and chartreuse are good colors to use. For the Bushwacker™, though, all colors are good. Flip it or draw it through the water, using an underhanded cast. Toss it into holes and around structure, and vary the retrieve.

Shallow Water and Crankbaits

In shallow water, the crankbaits made by Rebel™ or Rapala™ are perfect. The jointed or broken-backs, as they are popularly known, are most effective. They should be from four to six inches in size, black with a white underside, or trout colored. These are used mainly in the spring and fall in the early morning and late afternoon.

You can troll one of these baits, or cast it hard and noisy or soft and gentle with a twitching motion after it lands. The faster you retrieve, the deeper it will run. A slow retrieve will keep it on the surface, a medium retrieve will run it down a couple of feet from the surface, and a fast retrieve will force it down for a deep run.

Deep Runners

The Rebel™ deep runners, the Flat Rake™, and the Crawfish Mudbug™ are sure bets for use as deep-running crankbaits. These should be in the four- to six-inch range, with purple backs and white bottoms. They are used mainly in the early spring when fish are down deep, on structure or

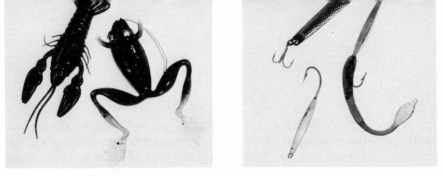

Rubber Baits   Jigs

drop-offs in 20-25 feet of water. The Bayley Big B™, the Natural Ike™, and the Lazy Ike™ will serve as confidence builders when using deep runners.

Keep on your toes when using deep runners, because you never know when the strike will occur. If you are near shallow water, you may see that deep V-wake that tells you that the bass has seen his target and is about to strike; in deep water, the signs are not so evident.

Jig and Eel

Jig and eels, jig and pork, and jig and worms are used in colder weather, and are fished with an underhanded flipping technique which creates a natural falling motion that drives bass crazy. The jig is really a spoon with a trailing hook on which a 3 inch rubber eel or worm or a piece of pork rind is attached. These are relatively new and effective lures, well worth experimenting with, especially on fall fishing trips.

Live Bait

Success with the use of live bait requires proper hooking of the bait. Live bait means just that — "live" bait. You cannot force a frog that is hooked improperly and half-dead to move, for instance. You must hook him properly, and he must move on his own for the most action.

You can create vibrations more readily with artificial lures designed to be tugged through the water on the end of a line; live bait must remain alive and "kicking" in order to be effective.

In the case of the frog, hook him through the large muscle of the back leg. This gives him free action of both legs. Whatever you do, don't hook him through the lip — he'll drown!

Shiners are hooked through the dorsal fin; be very careful not to hook into the backbone!

Crayfish are hooked through the top of the hard shell, not through the tail. The tail of the crayfish is what gives it the action, pulling it along backwards like a lobster.

Grasshoppers are hooked essentially the same way as crayfish, through the hard collar just in back of the head.

Any live baits should be hooked gently, with the idea of allowing maximum movement and longevity.

A Fishing Journal

Check out your different lures and baits, remembering which the bass prefer at different times of the day or season, and under different weather conditions. Presentation of the lure and the type of retrieve you use will vary with the weather conditions.

One very useful way to remember what worked well, and when, is to keep a journal of your fishing trips. Many successful fishermen keep a small journal in their tackle box. In the journal, a short synopsis of each trip is written, making note of weather conditions, temperature, water temperature, depth at which bass were biting, which lures worked best, etc. This journal (which can be written on a small note pad) is a useful memory jogger for the next time you fish that lake, or another lake under similar conditions. Each trip is a learning experience, and each subsequent trip will become a greater success if a journal is kept.

Nine times out of ten, you can turn an unproductive day into a learning event by thinking over what you did and what went wrong. In the same respect, when you have an exceptionally good day, note what you did right. There may have been one or two things you have changed in your approach that could be keys to improving your technique.

Remember your lakesites, the places you have caught bass in the past. Try new ones, but go back to the old tried and true spots to bring back your confidence before searching out the new sites once more.

Always be on the lookout for the telltale sign that bass are present. A V-shaped, slow-moving wake or swirl, or maybe the twitching of the lily pads, or even the erratic jumping of bait fish that look like they are being shot right out of the water two or three feet, can all be signals that mean that an old lunker is down there doing his thing.

That spirit of boldness, that assured attitude, that confidence that you will develop in yourself, are parts of your technique, too. If you know you have the ability to outsmart the bass, then you will boat your fair share of lunkers.

From the Bump to the Boat

What do you do when you get a hit? That little bump on the end of the line that means a bass has taken an interest in what you have to offer strikes fear and panic into many novices, causing them to lose good fish.

If you are using a treble hook lure, set the hook right away and *hard,* as hard as you can. Make sure there is no slack on the line, and pull up high with the rod.

If you are using a rubber worm, let him run four or five feet with it. This may require a few seconds — don't be impatient. After he has run with the

Set the hook hard, and keep his head high!

worm he will roll it up in a ball in his mouth; now is the time to set the hook, as if there were a world record on the other end of that line!

Once the hook is set, do you horse him in fast, or do you play the bass depending on his weight and size? Your judgment in each case can help you boat the fish or cause you to yank the hook out of the soft part of his mouth because you did not set it successfully.

You will be able to tell if the bass is of any size at all if you are using a bass rod with a strong bony back and a sensitive tip. Bass that are very large will not move off very fast. Small bass hit with a vengeance and run very fast for the nearest obstacle to shake off the lure or worm.

If you know you have a very large bass on the line — and you *will* know — work him through or around obstacles and try to get his head above water. Keep the rod high and the line taut.

When bringing the bass in to the boat, keep his nose up. If his nose is down, you won't be able to get a net under him, or your hand in his gill rake, to lift him aboard.

The type of net you are using can make a big difference. A bass net is usually 26 inches across with a 24- or 36-inch sturdy handle. There have been numerous occasions when we have seen novices lose nice fish by trying to stuff a big bass into a net designed for trout fishing.

From shore bring a bass in so he is lying on his side, and net him as quickly as possible.

If you are going to turn your bass loose, keep him out of the water as little time as possible. That thin membrane on his outer surface keeps fungus from forming; if it is damaged by too much handling, the bass will eventually die.

Shore Fishing

If you have the stalking ability of an Indian, the cunning of a coon, and the eye of an eagle, then fishing from shore will be a pleasure for you. Otherwise, we recommend that you do most of your bass fishing from a boat. Still, there *can* be a whole different and worthwhile approach to bassing from shore, especially in the early spring when the flies begin to hatch and smallmouth are jumping for their breakfast. Fly fishing for bass from shore can be a challenge, and sometimes one of the best fishing treats, especially in such areas as the Wachusett Reservoir in central Massachusetts where boats are not allowed. The Wachusett, though noted for its trout, has some record-breaking smallmouth within its confines, and fly fishing for these little monsters is a great deal of fun.

First, check along the shallows for bait fish. If bass fingerlings are present, then bass are surely in the area. Second, find the telltale signs of a bass lair. Look for logs, overhangs, large rocks, weed flats, and submerged structure.

When you approach an area to fish, try to come in on the sunny side, facing the sun. Doing this will prevent you from casting a shadow in the water that might spook the fish.

When fly fishing, use a large bushy fly or brightly-colored bass bug. Clipped deer hair bugs, cricket bugs, spiders, grasshoppers, frog pattern bugs, the Muddler Minnow, Wooly Worm, and the Marabou Streamer are all effective fly fishing baits.

If not fly fishing, live bait — particularly shiners, crayfish, helgrammites, and night crawlers — is your best bet when fishing from shore. Sometimes you will find it helpful to wade into the shallows around weed beds. Stealth is the key to this approach, however; move as slowly and quietly as possible.

Night Fishing

Fishing at night requires different techniques than daytime angling. Bass come in around docks, shallows, and other places that are usually too active during the day. They come in to shore to hunt for their natural prey — frogs, crayfish, and large night insects.

We generally try to fish at night only when there is sufficient moonlight. Otherwise, we carry a couple of high intensity lanterns or electric lamps inside the boat. The trouble with the use of artificial light is that it makes it difficult to maintain night vision.

Know where your partner is trying to fish. It is normally a gentleman's agreement that the guy in front of the boat has 180 degrees from one side to the other. The man in the back of the boat has about the same amount of territory, only he will be fishing from right to left a little more often.

As night falls, get out the topwater noise baits and fish the shoreline around docks, logs, brush, and other structure.

At night, around the same structures where in the daytime we have picked up one- or two-pounders, we have boated five- or six-pounders. *Noise* is the key to night fishing. Use Jitterbugs™, wide spinners, Hula Poppers™, Rebels™ with broken backs, Bush Hogs™ — any bait that you can run out on the lily pads, in the shallows, around structure, or really thrash around on the surface.

Experimentation

Not all of us are going to have super bass fishing days all the time. Do not let yourself get down after coming in empty-handed from a full day of fishing. Those days will get fewer and farther between as you develop your own technique and ability to change methods rapidly.

You have to be flexible, trying different baits and using different methods. Every experience you have will give you new insight. Maybe you will remember that last week this did not work. Try it again; if it doesn't work this time, you will know to change quickly.

If the partner in the boat with you is using what you think is an improper technique, try to suggest new ways and methods that he may not be familiar with — but always encourage, never discourage. Remember, the learning process is the greatest aid in developing technique. Keep notes in your memory or on paper. Learn from your experiences, both good and bad.

Experiment! Do not be afraid to try new things. The bass may change their habits for any given day, reason, or condition. We have to learn to take our techniques and change them, add to them, or subtract from them. Whatever is going to benefit you in your endeavor of getting that lunker to the side of the boat is worth investigating — including creating a *new* technique.

New England's natural beauty, and good fisheries, are well worth preserving.

CHAPTER **5**

CONSERVATION

Keeping your catch alive — catch-and-release philosophy — bass fishing clubs — conservation policies and regulations — acid rain in New England.

One of man's most unnatural habits is waste. This is becoming more and more evident every day as we discover the shocking evidence of destruction all over the planet.

Preservation of as much of nature as possible for our children and grandchildren is one of the most important and deep-seated issues of our times. People may well be in the process of destroying the very earth we depend upon for our existence. But with just a little effort by each of us this could truly be a "garden of Eden".

As bass men we try to teach and practice the art of keeping our catch alive, either in a live well or by just returning the fish to the lake as quickly as possible.

There is not anything that turns an angler's stomach more than to see fish floating belly up on a lake or pond due to someone's disregard for life. This often happens when someone catches one or two fish and, instead of taking them home, just throws them in the woods or back in the water. This can be prevented by using a live well. They are not that expensive. A homemade rig can be set up for under $50, including batteries for the pump.

The live well consists of a large cooler or water-proof box, a pump to circulate the water, a 12-volt battery to run the pump, and four or five gallons of water from the lake or river in which you are fishing.

Put the water in the tank just after you catch the first fish you intend to keep, then turn on the pump every 20 minutes or so to aerate the water until you have caught your limit.

The live well can be portable or part of your boat's fixtures. To preserve nature, invest a little time and money.

Stringers should only be used with the intention of keeping the catch to eat. Bass cannot breathe on a stringer. Special nets made for keeping your catch over the side of the boat are more nuisance than they are worth, getting caught in weeds, confining and jostling the fish, and hurting the chances of a healthy return to the lake.

Out of 30,000 fingerlings that may hatch in one nest, only 10-15 survive to be five-pounders and only two or three survive to the seven- to nine-pound range. No more than 100 survive beyond the first year. So, as you can see, an entire population of bass could easily be exterminated if everyone ignored state catch limits and allowed their catch to die from neglect or ignorance.

If you are not going to use your catch for food, *keep them alive* to insure future generations of fishermen the exciting challenge of hunting the black bass.

Handle your fish as little as possible before releasing.

Releasing Fish Properly

Many fishermen are so careless in handling their catches that many released fish die. Guidelines for proper catch and release techniques have been developed from information obtained from fisheries studies. They are:

1. Use artificial lures whenever possible. Natural baits are usually swallowed deeply by bass causing damage to the gills or heart of the fish.

2. Set the hook quickly when using live bait or treble-hooked lures, spinners, etc., to prevent the fish sucking in the lure deeply.

3. Land the fish as quickly as possible. There are times when a fish must be played, particularly larger ones, but, unless you plan on eating your catch, be careful not to tease a fish to exhaustion and shock.

4. Grab a bass by the lower jaw when boating and removing hooks. This reduces handling of the fish. Never hold a fish by grasping by the eyes. This can cause blindness and cause damage to its nervous system.

5. If the bass is gut hooked — *do not remove the hook!* Cut the line and release the fish. Most fish hooked in the throat or gills will die after the hook is removed, but acidic fluids in the fish will dissolve the hook away within weeks and the fish will feed normally as long as it is not injured by yanking or tearing the hook out.

6. Release the fish into the water gently. Tossing it in can cause internal injuries.

7. Once a fish has been placed on a stringer *take it home.* Do not attempt to release it; chances are that exhaustion and stress will have already taken their toll.

Support Your Local Bass Club

Local bass club chapters have been instrumental in promoting our natural resources. Bass clubs work with youth groups, in acid rain education programs, on lake and launch site improvements, and help lobby for laws and regulations that will help protect bass fishing resources for the future. Also, recent technological advances in fishing equipment are due, in part, to bass anglers' interest in improving their sport.

In the past there have been fears that tournaments held by bass clubs were cleaning out bass populations in lakes. The fears are unfounded in that all fish are released and are sometimes even tagged to help state agencies in bass studies. There are also severe penalties for dead fish brought in during a tournament, with heavy weight penalties subtracted from the score.

Support of your local club or group can be an interesting learning experience that helps you do your part in conserving our natural resources.

Regulations

Special regulations are designed to protect or promote specific species to maximize the harvest, protect spawning, impose size limits to insure growth to maturity, prevent over-fishing, and promote recreational rather than consumptive use. As with any government program, there will be laws and regulations with which you may not agree. Make sure you understand the desired effect a regulation is designed to produce. Educate yourself, and get involved.

Too many times we've seen local residents of a lake or pond who believe they know fish ecology better than their fish and game department. They may take matters into their own hands by introducing species they desire to a water and disregarding regulations. These tactics are most often harmful to long-term plans for fisheries, are wasteful and counter-productive.

Acid Rain

The Quabbin Reservoir in western Massachusetts is the largest tract of wildland in that state, and may soon be fishless unless sufficient steps are taken to control acid rain pollution. The Quabbin has been the site of some of the best bass fishing in New England, and we hope that this grand body of water, and others affected, will be saved.

Recent experiments with trout, which, along with smallmouth bass and walleyes, are always the first species to be affected by pH level changes, were conducted by the Division of Fisheries and Wildlife. It was determined that fish placed at the mouths of streams feeding the Quabbin on the western side died from the effects of acidification.

Acid rain, as we have been experiencing it here in Massachusetts, is the result of the conversion of airborne pollutants, primarily sulfur oxides and nitrogen oxides in the upper atmosphere, into sulfuric and nitric acids which fall to earth in rain, snow, fog and as dry fallout.

The precipitation that carries these pollutants in their converted form is abnormally acidic. Acidity is measured on a scale from zero to fourteen, called the pH. Seven on this scale is neutral, below seven is acidic, and higher than seven is alkaline. A small difference in pH scale is, in reality, a large difference in acidity. A pH of four is 10 times as acidic as a pH of five and 100 times as acidic as that of six, and so forth.

Normal, unpolluted rain has a pH of about 5.6. In 1981, the average pH of rainfall in Massachusetts was 4.1 and in 1982 the average pH dropped to 3.85.

The possible effects of acid rain read like a horror story. Fish kills, extinction of whole species of fish, reduction in tree productivity, leaching of lead and copper from pipes into drinking water, accelerated corrosion of

Catch-and-release will preserve our fishing heritage for future generations.

manmade structures, are just a few. Add decreasing visibility, contamin-
ated fish and water affecting human health, accumulation of mercury or
pesticides in fish, the build-up of lead in soils, and human death and disease
from the inhalation of sulfates and other fine particles in the atmosphere,
and it's obvious the concerned angler should support research and regulations dealing with this issue.

The major sources of this pollution are coal-burning power plants, industrial boilers, and automobiles. The Ohio Valley area is one of the biggest
sulfur emitting producers directly affecting the northeast and Canada.
Many members of Congress have claimed that there has not been a sufficient
outcry from fishermen and conservationists to promote increased pollution
controls. This is an area where every angler should get involved and make
himself heard. It is disturbing to consider the result of silence on the part
of sportsmen and conservationists on the future of this beautiful and
bountiful bass fishing region.

The United States and Canada have agreed to work toward a solution
to this problem; in the meantime, bass fishermen can let legislators know
that we care about preserving our natural resources for future generations.

CHAPTER **6**

ICE FISHING

Ice fishing techniques — laying out the lake in advance — using topographical maps — finding the comfort range — bait.

Why stop fishing for bass when the lake freezes over? Very few bass anglers consider the sport of bassing through the ice as being worth the trouble; ice fishing for bass *is* a specialized art. But with the proper bait and a little planning fishing for the largemouth and smallmouth bass through the New England ice can be very rewarding, and a lot of fun.

There is much debate among ice fishermen as to whether bass strike in deep water. Some believe that bass mud the bottom in winter, and are not interested in other food because their bodily functions have slowed down to a state of semi-hibernation. This is an excellent excuse for coming home empty-handed, but the truth is bass are seeking a comfort zone where the oxygen content and temperature are more suited to them. Bass comfort zones differ from those of coldwater fish, and you have to think like a bass undergoing a New England winter to catch bass under the ice.

In the period from November to late December, after fall fishing has ended and the ice is setting in, check out your equipment. You will need a hand or power auger, tilt-ups, hooks, lines, warm winter clothing and boots, and a box sled for transporting the gear over the ice.

The auger should be well sharpened; if it's a power auger, tune the engine. Spools should be oiled with vegetable oil, which will not harm the water or the fish. Lines should be checked, and frayed lines changed. In short, make sure everything is in proper working order.

At this time, also begin looking over topographic maps of the lakes you will be fishing. The drop-offs, shallows, and bottom structure, and a wealth of other information, is contained in these maps.

Start out by selecting a small pond, from 50 to 70 acres, that you know as a good bass producer during the open water season. Figure 1 (see page 59) is an example of a simple topographical layout of such a pond, showing the water depths and some outstanding features that can be used as visual reference points.

Ice fishing starts with making a hole with chisel or auger.

We can determine from this map that the bass will probably frequent the 30 feet deep swale which crosses the lake bottom. We know that bass will be seeking a comfort layer where the water temperature is warmest and the oxygen supply is adequate. A thermal layer, where the temperature is between 39 and 42 degrees, probably exists near the bottom. The bass will also avoid very deep holes, because the water there may lack adequate oxygen. They may feed in these deep areas, but will return quickly to the thermal layer.

Choose three possible areas to explore, and circle them on the map. In figure 2, Area 1 is situated on a steep drop-off; note the hillside which runs in a banking of rocks into the water and quickly drops from 10 feet to 18 feet, to 26 feet, then to 30 feet. This area will make it easy to fish different depths to determine exactly where old mossy-back and his cousins are feeding.

We chose Area 2 because, although it does not drop off as sharply, it does drop to the 30-foot depth over a bed of rocks. Area 3, though quite near the shallows, is also deep and close to possible food supplies.

Having chosen the sites we will use for our set-ups, we mark off the approximate length in feet from the point of entry onto the pond to our three areas, taking into consideration several reference points — the hill, the dam, the rushes, etc.

Upon entering the pond on our first trip, we examine it carefully. At this point, we will zero in on the center of the right side of the pond. There is the hill — as marked on the map. It is steep and rocky. Area 1 could very well be the place where bass are waiting!

We head right, about 100 yards, to the foot of the hill and a large outcrop of rock, then turn toward the lake and head straight out about 50 to 60 feet.

If our calculations are correct we should be standing over Area 1. Now we dig five holes in a semi-circle and drop a mercury thermometer on a line, which is knotted every 10 feet for depth estimation, until it reaches bottom, and take the temperature. We then drop the thermometer to a level 5 to 10 feet above bottom and take the temperature again. We repeat the procedure, lifting the thermometer 5 to 10 feet each time, until we find the favored 39- to 42-degree thermal layer.

Once the proper thermal layer is found, we then set our tip-ups by each hole. Tip-ups, or tilt-ups, are handy items which hold the line, spool, etc.; they are spring-loaded, so that when a bass strikes, a flag snaps up as a signal.

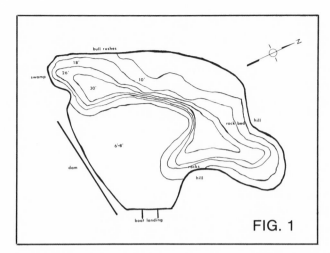

First, check a contour map.

FIG. 1

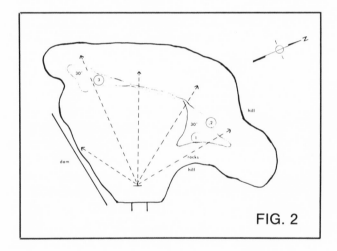

Next, pick the site that offers the proper bottom structure and depth.

FIG. 2

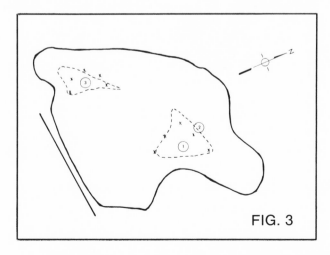

Last, locate five holes around the top sites, and try your luck!

FIG. 3

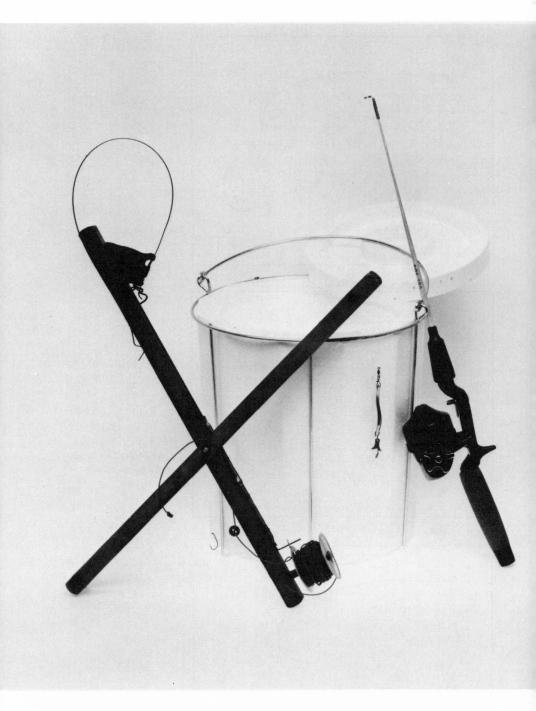

Ice fishing equipment: tip-up, minnow bucket, and jigging pole.

Using a sounder attached to the hook, we drop our line to the bottom, then raise it to the proper depth. In this case, the 14-foot depth is the proper thermal layer to start our hunt for bass. We slide a button marker up to mark the depth on our fishing line.

Next, we select our bait. Experience teaches that the best bait for bass fishing through the ice is a shiner — the larger, the better! The five-inch shiner seems to be the ultimate temptation for these now sluggish fish.

Hook the shiner gently through its back, just behind its fin. Alternately, some fishermen hook shiners through the tail. The more lively the shiner, the more action will result, so don't mangle the bait any more than necessary during hooking.

After lowering the bait to the level marked on the line, go to the next hole and repeat the process. The holes are set out in a semi-circle 20 feet apart; we sit in a location in the middle of these for the best view of the flags.

All rigged up now, we can sit back with a hot cup of coffee and wait. The action is usually fast; but if, after about 15 or 20 minutes, nothing happens, check the tilts and baits. Raise or lower some of the baits. Sometimes just a six- to eight-inch movement can cause a bass to strike. If Area 1 proves to be unproductive, move the whole set-up to Area 2 or 3 the next time you fish the pond. It is very important (1) to find the thermal layer that largemouth and smallmouth prefer, and (2) to use large shiners which will attract bass.

When you do catch some bass, keep them fresh by putting them in snow — or drill another hole, string them on a lead, and stake them in the hole.

Dress warmly, from head to toe. That old north wind can cut through you like a knife. There is no worse fishing trip than one for which you are ill-prepared, and the trick to catching bass in winter is to be well prepared. Good luck, and many flags to you!

Handle your bass with care from pond to pan and you'll have a meal to remember!

CHAPTER **7**

THE PALATE PLEASIN' BASS

Caring for your catch, from pond to pan —
cleaning — some favorite New England recipes.

The bass, along with most other fish, is high in protein and low in calories making it not only pleasing to your palate, but also an outstanding organic and nutritional addition to anyone's diet. The hours spent on the lakes and rivers of New England in search of the notorious black bass will culminate in one of the best taste treats to be found anywhere.

Bass is a versatile food, and can be used in a variety of dishes for a variety of occasions — from a quick family meal to a tasty sample that will be sure to please the guests at your next party.

The first step to preparing your fish is the cleaning process. This can be quick and easy, and you can avoid the usual mess by following the steps below.

There are two ways to clean bass: (1) scaling and preparing the whole fish for stuffing, and (2) filleting the fish without having to scale it — this produces two fine fillets. The utensils required are a rounded-edge knife for scaling and a fine, thin-bladed knife for filleting.

To clean the *whole* fish, first remove all the scales by running the rounded-edge knife against the grain — from the tail forward — on both sides and around the fins, using a lot of water to help remove the scales. The more water you use to rinse the fish, the better.

Next, with the filleting knife, cut around the girth of the body, just in front of the fin and behind the gills, and cut through the neck bone to remove the head. Slide the knife to the very inside of the stomach wall, right down to the rear of the fish, to the aperture where the stomach ends. Lay back the stomach wall, remove the intestines, remove the bladder, and open the inner skin layer, a very fine membrane that holds back the pressure of the water. You will find a very small coagulation of blood at the base of the stomach, next to the backbone. Remove this by scraping it away with your fingers or the edge of the knife.

Put the cleaned fish in a large pan of cold water, add about two tablespoons of salt, and let soak for about two hours. This removes the remaining blood from the body, resulting in a very fine white, delicate piece of fish.

Preparing the Whole Fish

1: Remove the scales.

4: Fold back the stomach walls.

2: Sever the head.

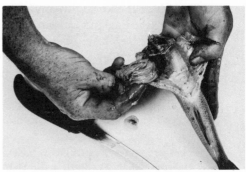

5: Remove the internal organs.

3: Slide the knife to where the stomach ends.

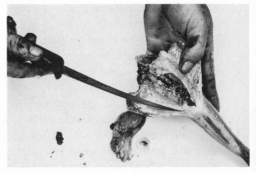

6: Rinse with clean water.

Filleting the Fish

1: Run the knife along both sides
   of the back fin.

3: Insert knife at the original cut
   and slide along backbone and
   rib cage.

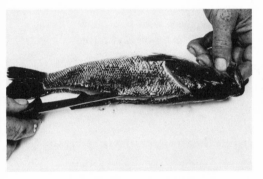

2: Insert the knife just under the
   layer of skin and roll back.

4: Cut the fillet away.

The *filleting* process is a bit more difficult — with this method, you are actually removing the meat from the bones. First, run your filleting knife along both sides of the back fin, the full length of the body, from the back of the head right to the tip of the tail. (You do not have to remove the scales from the fish to fillet it.) Once you have made these two cuts, insert your knife just under the layer of the skin and roll the skin down toward the stomach and down along the back to the tail so that the skin on both sides will lay open right to the stomach. Then insert your knife back in along your original cut. Slide your knife along the backbone on both sides, then along the rib cage until you reach the stomach area. You can feel the large bones that run from the backbone to the stomach area as you cut the meat away from them.

After you have removed the two fillets, soak them, as before, to obtain a very delicate white fish, similar to haddock or schrod.

Now you are ready to prepare your bass for the table. Carl Apperson, along with his talents as a bass fisherman, is also an excellent cook. The following recipes are from his personal files and are favorites of his family and friends.

Salt and Pepper Broiled Bass

Three to four bass fillets   pinch salt
¼ lb. butter   pinch pepper
1 fresh lemon   light dusting paprika

Bring your broiler up to heat. Lay the fillets on a large sheet pan. Take half the butter and drop it on the bass fillets in small chips. Sprinkle the fillets with salt and pepper. Broil on one side for three to four minutes, then turn the pieces over. Dot with the rest of the butter and sprinkle with salt and pepper. Put a few drops of lemon juice on each fillet and broil for another three to four minutes. Just before they're done, sprinkle them with paprika and broil for another minute. Serve hot with white sauce, or lemon and butter sauce. Serves four.

Deep Fried Bass Fillets

Three to four bass fillets
Batter made of milk, egg, salt and pepper
Dry batter made of Golden Dip^{TM} and white flour (or your favorite bread
    crumb mixture with flour)

Cut your fillets into eight-ounce servings. Dry them off and lay them in the milk and egg mixture. Soak them well, then put them into the Golden Dip^{TM} and flour mixture and let them sit in the refrigerator for 30 to 40 minutes.

Take them out and drop them into the heated oil in your fryer one at a time. When the piece of fillet starts to float, remove it and put it on a drying rack in the oven at 200 degrees. This will drain any excess oil from the deep frying process. Serve piping hot with french fries or hot potatoes and vegetables. Serves four.

New England Bass Chowder

Three to four pounds of   ½ oz. fresh parsley
    fresh cubed bass fillets   ⅛ oz. salt
2 lbs. fine diced potatoes   1/16 oz. white pepper
1 large white onion, diced   2 quarts heavy cream
4 oz. whole corn, fresh (or canned   1/16 oz. poultry seasoning
    when out of season)   ¼ lb. butter
                                 1 c. white wine (optional)

Put cubed fish into a saucepan with one-quarter cup of water; cook until tender.

Bring potatoes, diced onions, corn, parsley to a boil in two cups of water. When the fish is tender, add it, and the water in which it was cooked, to the potatoes, onions, and corn. Add salt and white pepper. Bring this up to heat; add poultry seasoning for just a touch of added flavor. Just before this starts to simmer, add heavy cream and butter. Add one cup of white wine (or water, if you prefer); simmer for 20 minutes. Serve piping hot with garlic bread and a fresh garden salad. Serves 8 to 10.

Baked Stuffed Bass

One large bass, four to five lbs.,
   or two smaller bass, two to
   three pounds each, scaled and
   cleaned (not filleted)
2 lbs. stuffing bread
3 stalks celery
1 medium onion

$\frac{1}{8}$ tsp. Italian seasoning
$\frac{1}{8}$ tsp. poultry seasoning
One 8 oz. can medium oysters
1 c. cream or milk
2-3 eggs
Salt and pepper

Cut up the onion and celery and saute in a pan with Italian and poultry seasonings. Add oysters and their juice; saute for two or three minutes.

Break the hard stuffing bread up in a bowl. Add one cup of water and the sauteed ingredients and mix, then eggs (to hold the stuffing together) and mix again.

Stuff the prepared fish. Add salt and pepper to top of fish and place in a pan. Put $\frac{1}{2}$ cup water in bottom of the pan and add a cup of cream or milk. Bake in 375-degree oven until done (approximately 15 minutes per pound). Serves 6.

Baked Stuffed Bass with Crabmeat

Follow the previous recipe but substitute eight-ounce can of shredded crabmeat for oysters. Mix juice and all into the stuffing. There is no need to saute the crabmeat.

Boston Bass Casserole

2-3 lbs. bass fillets in $\frac{1}{4}$"-$\frac{1}{2}$" chunks
Pasta (egg noodles or your
   favorite pasta)
$\frac{1}{4}$ c. butter
$\frac{1}{2}$ c. green pepper

$\frac{1}{2}$ c. carrots
1 tsp. parsley
1 clove garlic
1 can cream of mushroom soup

Cook egg noodles as directed, drain, and add a little butter so they will not stick.

Roll the bass chunks in drawn butter, then saute them in a pan. Take green peppers and carrots (cut julienne style), parsley, and garlic and simmer until tender. Then add bass chunks and simmered vegetables to the egg noodles in a casserole dish. Add a can of cream of mushroom soup and mix. Bake until it sets up well. Serves 4-6.

Sweet and Sour Bass Tidbits

2-3 lbs. bass fillets in 1" chunks
A fondue set-up with a light cooking oil, 375 degrees
Five different dips, either hot or cold (recipes follow):
    Cheese Sauce
    Mustard Sauce
    Garlic White Sauce
    Lemon Sauce
    Sweet and Sour Sauce
    Ground Relish Sauce

Put a bass chunk in the cooking oil and cook to your preference, usually two to three minutes; remove and dip into, or spoon on, one of the six sauces, each in its own dish.

This great party dish serves 8.

Basic White Sauce

4 Tbsp. butter   ¼ tsp. pepper
4 Tbsp. flour   2 c. milk
½ tsp. salt

Melt butter in saucepan. Blend in flour, salt, and pepper. Stir until mixture is smooth and bubbling. Remove from heat. Stir in milk, then return to heat and stir constantly until boiling. Boil about one minute, stirring.

Cheese Sauce

Add about 1 c. of your favorite cheese (cheddar is great!) and ½ tsp. dry mustard to the white sauce. Stir until the grated cheese is well melted.

Mustard Sauce

Add mustard, dry or prepared, to the white sauce, to taste.

Garlic White Sauce

Add 1 or 2 crushed cloves of garlic to the white sauce.

Lemon Sauce

2 Tbsp. cornstarch	2 Tbsp. sugar (or to taste)
1 c. water	¼ tsp. salt
½ c. lemon juice or	⅛ tsp. pepper
¼ c. concentrate	A bay leaf, if you desire

Mix cornstarch, water, and lemon juice until smooth. Add salt, pepper, and bay leaf. Bring to a boil over medium heat, stirring constantly. Boil for one minute.

Sweet and Sour Sauce

To the lemon sauce, add pineapples, sauteed green peppers and onions, and 1 Tbsp. of vinegar. If you desire, add also a bit of ginger, garlic, a tablespoon of butter, and soy sauce for a tangier sauce.

Ground Relish Sauce

Put ½ c. pickles or pickle relish, ¼ c. green pepper, 1 clove garlic, 1 tsp. salt, ¼ c. celery, and 1 Tbsp. parsley in a blender and grind to a fine consistency.

CHAPTER **8**

CONNECTICUT

Candlewood Lake — Lake Lillinonah — Pachaug
Pond — Gardner Lake — Quaddick Reservoir —
Mashapaug Lake — Rogers Lake — other
favorites by county.

The Nutmeg State offers New England fishermen the experience of "southern" fishing in the Northeast. Connecticut's bass fishing waters are similar to, and have sizable fish like Virginia and the Carolinas. The Gulf Stream runs in and curves out off the coast of Connecticut, causing a temperature increment of 6 to 10 degrees in the winter and 10 to 15 degrees in the summer. No other state but Florida catches the Gulf Stream fully along its coast; it's almost like going 600 miles south to fish for largemouth.

Connecticut has above-average bass fishing (to help scratch that bass fishing itch!) from the Connecticut River Valley area, where tobacco is grown along the banks, to the Rhode Island and Massachusetts borders.

Candlewood — Connecticut's Western Wonder

Candlewood Lake, in western Connecticut, lies along Route 7 near the New York State border. Fifty years ago there was no lake here, just beautiful scenic farmland. Today, a 5,600-acre lake stretches 11 miles long with a maximum width of nearly two miles. According to the Department of Environmental Protection, Candlewood is "definitely one of the top lakes in the state."

From late April to early May, bass fishing is excellent. Three- to four-pounders are common, and the lake is filled with trophy-sized largemouth and smallmouth.

Jig and Pig seems to be the bait of choice on Candlewood since Art Singer, a well-known fisherman in the area and winner of the 1981 Northeastern Bass Association's championship, introduced that bait to local fishermen. Flipping for bass on Candlewood has become quite popular. Just flip your lure in short casts around structure such as stumps, logs, and the like; retrieve slowly. Black and purple-colored jellyworms are also excellent baits to use here.

Candlewood Lake is the home of many trophy bass.

The Sherman and Brookfield areas of the lake are noted for bass action. Two public boat launchings are operated by the state. One is located at Squantz Pond State Park on Route 39 in New Fairfield; the other is located in Lattin's Cove in Danbury, off Pocono Point Road. Occasionally, the water level is so low that these ramps are unusable, so check ahead if you are planning on launching a fairly large boat.

There are several tackle shops in the area where you can obtain the latest information on the lake's hotspots and recently successful lures. Hank's Tackle Shop, Germantown Road, Danbury; White's Fish and Tackle Shop, Candlewood Corners, Route 39, New Fairfield; and Garrison Firearms, Federal Road, Brookfield are a few.

A good map of Candlewood can be obtained from the International Map Company, 595 Broad Ave., Ridgefield, NJ 07657. Call (201) 943-5550 for current prices.

Lake Lillinonah

Lake Lillinonah, a hydroelectric impoundment located on the Housatonic River in Newtown, Brookfield, Bridgewater, and Southbury, is one of the best bass producing lakes in Connecticut.

Lillinonah is deep (100-plus feet), and covers just under 2,000 acres. Super bass are taken each year by average fishermen and professionals alike, some ranging in the six- to nine-pound range.

Recent studies have found that Lake Lillinonah has abundant numbers of fast-growing largemouth bass. A good population of smallmouth exists, also, as well as a fine, healthy population of the scrappy little calico bass.

Lake Lillinonah has good fishing all season, but is exceptionally good in the fall around the shallows. Fish this area with jellyworms, eels, and the like, for some fine action.

Gardner Lake

If smallmouth are your preference, then Gardner Lake, located in the towns of Salem, Montville, and Boxrah, is the place to visit. This 487-acre lake has a maximum depth of 43 feet and a sandy, gravelly, and somewhat rubbly bottom scattered with boulders. This is the kind of environment that smallmouth love. There is some weed cover in the shallows and a few areas of muddy bottom, but the majority of the area is gravel.

There is plenty of well-oxygenated water here, and the smallmouth are abundant and grow well. The shoreline is moderately developed. There is a state-owned boat launching facility located on the southeastern shore.

Although Gardner Lake is noted for the trophy smallmouth taken from it in past years, there are also some pretty good largemouth here.

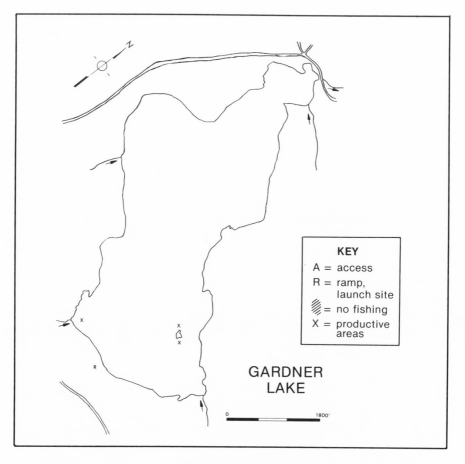

KEY

A = access
R = ramp, launch site
▨ = no fishing
X = productive areas

GARDNER LAKE

0   1800'

Pachaug Pond

Located in Griswold, Pachaug Pond lies just east of Exit 85 on the Connecticut turnpike. Most of this lake is less than 10 feet deep and filled with trophy sized largemouth.

Fish dark-colored jellyworms rigged weedless in and around brush piles and underwater creek beds. The bass fishing here is good all day long and all season. A plastic frog tossed in and around the weed growth is a sure enticement to old bucketmouth. One of the best areas of the pond to pick up some of those mama hawgs is in the area where the Pachaug River enters the lake.

As an added incentive for a visit to Pachaug Pond, there are no less than a dozen smaller ponds and lakes with great bass fishing within a 20-minute drive.

For more information on facilities in the area, contact the Norwich Chamber of Commerce, 1 Thames Plaza, Norwich, 06360, or call (203) 887-1647.

Pachaug Marina offers everything for your boating and fishing needs, as well as camping facilities. Write Pachaug Marina, RFD #3, Box 258, Norwich, 06360, or call (203) 376-3346.

Quaddick Reservoir

Landlocked alewives provide the forage that makes the largemouth in Quaddick Reservoir fat and scrappy. This 467-acre reservoir has a maximum depth of 25 feet and is really three basins separated by causeways. The lower and middle ponds have little vegetation, but there is fairly dense growth of submerged weeds in the upper basin, known as Stump Pond.

The bottom is composed mostly of sand and rubble — and some swamp ooze. There is moderate shoreline development, including a state-owned launching area located in Quaddick State Park.

Black crappie, otherwise known as calico bass, are all over the reservoir, and provide an interesting fishing experience. Largemouth are abundant, and there are some smallmouth here, too.

The weedless rigged jellyworm works well here, as in all places that have weedy coves; Quaddick has many little coves to explore.

Mashapaug Lake

Mashapaug Lake, located in Union, has given up several trophy-sized largemouth and smallmouth in recent years. This is the location from which the state record largemouth was taken in 1961 — a 12-pound 14-oz. lunker! This is a natural body of water with the water level raised by an earthen dam at its outlet. Due to industrial use of the water, the level does fluctuate to a degree, but the 297-acre lake has an average depth of nine feet with a maximum depth of 43 feet.

Most of the shallows have a bottom composed of sand, gravel, and rubble with scattered boulders. There is some emergent weed growth in some of the shallows, but in most other areas the bottom is mostly swampy. Mashapaug is clear and has good oxygen supply to about the 30-foot depth.

The launching area, state-owned, is located in Bigelow Hollow State Park at the southern end of the lake. There is a five-horsepower limit on outboards in Mashapaug.

Because of light development and a shoreline that is mostly hilly and forested, this is a quiet scenic lake to fish, so concentrate on bringing in a lunker here and your chances are good.

Rogers Lake

Located in the towns of Lyme and Old Lyme, this 265-acre lake is a real treat. Rogers has been stocked with all kinds of bass — largemouth, calico bass, rock bass, smallmouth and even striped bass. Landlocked alewives provide the forage base that keep these gamefish fat and healthy. An occasional calico has been reeled in that weighs in the two-and-a-half-pound range, and trophy-sized largemouth are taken every year.

Rogers has a maximum depth of 66 feet, and all but the very deepest water has good oxygen content. Submerged vegetation is thick in the shoal areas, and the bottom varies between mud, sand, gravel and rubble. The shoreline is well developed but thickly wooded, keeping it aesthetically pleasing.

Access to the lake is provided by a state-owned right-of-way and boat launching on the eastern shore of the lake.

Fishing the steep drop-offs in the northern part of the western shoreline with deep runners during summer will net you some surprises. There is a small 30-foot deep pool in the northeastern area of the lake that also attracts bass during cooler weather. Fish the weedy shoals in spring with dark rubber worms for largemouth action.

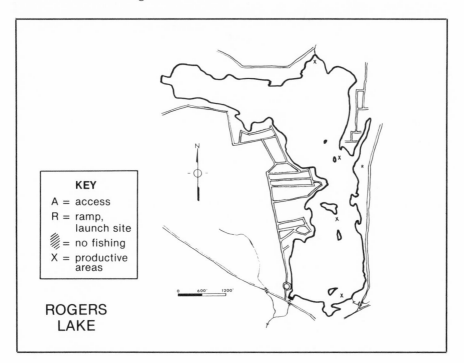

KEY

A = access
R = ramp, launch site
= no fishing
X = productive areas

ROGERS
LAKE

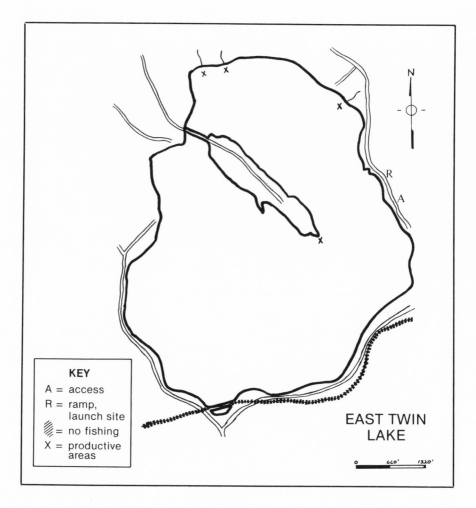

KEY

A = access
R = ramp,
 launch site
▨ = no fishing
X = productive
 areas

EAST TWIN
LAKE

0   660'   1320'

East Twin Lake

Located between Routes 41 and 44 in the town of Salisbury, East Twin Lake offers 562 acres of superb bass fishing. This is another of Connecticut's many waters that give up trophy-sized largemouths consistently. The maximum depth of East Twin is 80 feet; water is well-oxygenated and very clear. The lake is fed by many small brooks and numerous springs. These brooks, where they enter the lake, and the areas just off the springs are excellent places to fish surrounding structure if you are looking for a good fight with a trophy-sized lunker largemouth.

The northern area of the lake is very weedy. Because of East Twin's location in limestone country, acid rain has done little or no damage to its fisheries. Because the lake is so clear, bottom weeds grow at great depths allowing plenty of cover for bass; in fact, the fish can be *anywhere* on this lake, and finding them will take some keen tracking abilities.

In addition to large numbers of largemouth and some good smallmouth, rock bass are in good numbers in all shallow areas; there are some calico bass running loose here, too. Black and purple weedless jellyworms worked in the weedy shallows produce well; or try night fishing with dark-colored surface and noise baits.

There is one large boat livery on the eastern shore and a small state-owned right-of-way just south of the boat livery where car-top boats can gain access.

The Connecticut River

The Connecticut River extends from its mouth at Long Island Sound all the way to Canada, forming the natural boundary between New Hampshire and Vermont. The Connecticut River is covered in more depth in other chapters.

This great river, once threatened by pollution, now offers the best river fishing for bass in the New England region. From late April through June, fish the gravel bars and riffles for great smallmouth action. Both boat and shore fishing is available between Wilson and the Enfield Dam.

A public ramp access to the Enfield area is located on the western shore in Suffield. Rental boats are available in the Windsor Locks area.

As with any river that is used, in part, to produce hydroelectric power, there are many tricky places in the river — so be careful when boating! A good map of the river, some pre-planning, and common sense will make your tour of the Connecticut safe and enjoyable.

Other noteworthy bass waters

As with every New England state, there are many more bass waters in Connecticut, all worthy of mention, but it would take a book in itself to cover them all. We have selected some of the better bass waters, each followed with the necessary information. An especially important bass water will be preceded by an asterisk. A trip to any and all of these areas will please any bass fisherman, but do not forget to do some exploring on your own. A small mill pond in some small town may well surprise you; most New England ponds and rivers hold bass to some degree. New England is truly a bass fisherman's paradise, abounding with thousands of little Edens hidden across the beautiful landscape of this unique region of the country.

LITCHFIELD COUNTY

*Bantam Lake (Litchfield, Morris): Route 202; 916 acres, 25 feet maximum; eastern and western shores rocky; northern and southern shores weedy and flat; partially wooded and heavily developed shoreline; motors prohibited between the hours of 11:00 p.m. and 5 a.m.; large numbers of trophy sized LMB here; good SMB and calico bass action, too; heavy recreational use makes fishing more feasible in the early morning and late evening and at night.

Highland Lake (Winchester): off Route 44; 444 acres, 62 feet maximum; located in a high valley overlooking Winsted; fed by small brooks and bottom springs; weed flats in the upper shallow basin; few weedy areas in the other two basins; highly developed shoreline and heavy recreational use; access provided through a boat livery and a state-owned launching area; good SMB fishing as well as some LMB, calico bass and rock bass.

West Hill Pond (Barkhamsted, New Hartford): 238 acres, 59 feet maximum; sand, gravel and rubble bottom; vegetation is scarce and the water is clear; the main source of water is through bottom springs; good oxygen at deep levels; SMB fishing is good and there are some calico and rock bass, too; state-owned boat launching ramp and parking at the northern end adjacent to the dam.

Wononscopomuc Lake (Salisbury): off Route 44; 353 acres, 108 feet maximum; due to lack of oxygen fish do not survive below 35 feet; the town operates the boat livery and restricts fishing to 6:00 a.m. to 9 p.m.; the launching facility is located at the northeastern end of the lake and further restrictions in the hours that the livery is open restricts fishing even more; check locally on opening times before visiting Wononscopomuc, sometimes called Lakeville Lake; LMB, SMB, and rock bass are present in adequate numbers.

MIDDLESEX COUNTY

Cedar Lake (Chester): 68 acres, 45 feet maximum; sand, gravel and rubble bottom; in deeper areas the bottom is muddy. The lake is fed by bottom springs and Pataconk Brook; the shallow northern area of the lake is extremely weedy. The deeper areas are well oxygenated; light shoreline development and a picnic area and swimming area are located at the southeastern end of the lake; public access and boat launching are located at the northeastern end of the lake; there is good fishing for LMB here and some SMB as well as calico bass exist here.

Dooley Pond (Middletown): 28 acres, 16 feet maximum; fed by bottom springs and small brooks; bottom is mostly mud with some sand and gravel; this small pond is very weedy and almost completely choked with weeds on its southern end; during the warmer weather a thick algae bloom develops making this a good pond to fish very early in the season; public access and boat launching, as well as the entire pond, is state-owned; there should be some fairly good sized LMB here and bass fishing is good in spring.

Silver Lake — sometimes called Peat Works Pond (Berlin, Meriden): Route 15; 151 acres, 12 feet maximum; oozy bottom except for shallow shoreline which is gravelly; this lake is fed by springs and the headwaters of Belcher Brook; heavy weed growth in spring and intense algae bloom in late spring and early summer; light development; the Penn-Central Railroad borders the lake on the west and Route 15 parallels the lake on the east for about half a mile; public boat launching site is located at the northwestern end of the lake. There is fair to good LMB fishing here and some SMB action.

NEW HAVEN COUNTY

Black Pond (Meriden, Middlefield): 76 acres, 23 feet maximum; bottom is rock, gravel and mud in the shoals and ooze in the deeper areas; fed by bottom springs and surface runoff; shoal areas are very heavily weeded; there is good oxygen except in the deepest areas; light shoreline development; state-owned boat launching ramp at northeastern end of the pond and there is a boat livery, snack bar and bait shop at the northern end of the pond; the LMB are abundant and there are a good number of large bass with 5+ pounders not uncommon.

North Farms Reservoir (Wallingford): 62 acres, 5 feet maximum; gravel, rubble bottom covered with ooze; abundant submerged vegetation and dense algae blooms are common in warmer weather; this pond is state-owned and a boat launching is provided at the southeastern corner; use weedless rigged jellyworms for some excellent LMB fishing.

*Quonnipaug Lake (Guilford): Route 77; 112 acres, 48 feet maximum; fed by two small brooks and bottom springs; the shallow northern and southern areas of the lake are muddy and extremely weedy; the rest of the lake is sand and gravel bottom; good oxygen content in the deep cool water below the thermocline; public access provided through a boat livery at the southwestern end and a state-owned launching area at the northern end of the lake; landlocked alewives supply the forage that make the LMB fat and happy and willing to play; trophy sized bass are taken here often.

Candlewood Lake has been the site of many top bass tournaments.

NEW LONDON COUNTY

Amos Lake (Preston): 105 acres, 48 feet maximum; fed by brooks and springs; weedy in shallow area; clear water except in summer when there is a light algae bloom; mostly sand and gravel bottom; in summer the water below 22 feet suffers from lack of oxygen; state-owned boat launching on southwestern shore; fair fishing for LMB and SMB.

Beach Pond (Voluntown, Rockville, RI): 394 acres, 65 feet maximum; mostly sand, gravel, and rubble bottom; weeds are scarce and oxygen content is good; state-owned boat launching facility on northern shore of the pond; Rhode Island operates a state park at the eastern end of the pond; lots of SMB, LMB and calico bass though the sizes are somewhat small.

Billings Lake (North Stonington): 105 acres, 33 feet maximum; fed by springs with a sandy, gravelly bottom with boulders and ledge; some vegetation in shoal areas; state-owned boat launching area on northern end of lake; excellent fishing for SMB and there are some calico bass here, too.

Long Pond (Ledyard, North Stonington): 99 acres, 72 feet maximum; fed by Lantern Hill, Silex and three other unnamed brooks. Shoal areas have sand, gravel and rubble bottoms with some boulders; deeper areas are rubble, boulders and silt; weedy in shoal areas; the deeper northern basin is well oxygenated to 40 feet but the shallow southern basin suffers from lack of oxygen below 15 feet; state-owned boat launching on northeastern end of pond; moderate development and well-wooded shoreline; landlocked alewives provide excellent forage for the good number of trophy sized LMB here; there are some SMB and calicos, too.

*Moodus Reservoir (Moodus): south of Route 66; 451 acres, 10 feet maximum; there is a very healthy population of LMB here and Moodus gives up trophy bass regularly; access by a state-owned boat ramp.

Pataganset Lake (East Lyme): Route 51; 123 acres, 34 feet maximum; mostly wooded shoreline with a bottom of sand, gravel, rubble and mud; abundant weeds in the shallows and coves; the water is clear and there is little oxygen below 12 feet; state boat launching off Route 51 just west of Flanders; trophy sized calico bass are in abundance in this lake; LMB fishing is fair to good.

*Pickerel Lake (Colchester, East Haddam): 89 acres, 10 feet maximum; mostly muddy bottom with scattered areas of sand and gravel; emergent vegetation is scarce; submerged vegetation is abundant; the lake is fed by small brooks and springs; state-owned boat launching at the northern end of the lake; excellent fishing for LMB and calico bass.

TOLLAND COUNTY

*Crystal Lake (Ellington, Stafford): 201 acres, 50 feet maximum; some weeds confined to shallow area; mostly sand, gravel and boulders on the bottom; water is clear and there is good oxygen to 40 feet; SMB fishing here is excellent and the LMB fishing is good.

WINDHAM COUNTY

Black Pond (Woodstock): 73 acres, 23 feet maximum; moderately weedy shoal areas; bottom consists of sand, gravel, boulders and mud; the water is clear and oxygen is good to 20 feet; lightly developed shoreline and public access through state-owned boat launch; plenty of SMB here and some LMB.

Halls Pond (Eastford, Ashford): 82 acres, 14 feet maximum; weeds mostly confined to southwestern cove; the bottom is sand, gravel, rubble and overlain with mud in deeper areas; dark colored stained water; light shoreline development; access is limited and only small boats can be launched from the dam; LMB fishing fair and SMB fishing very good.

CHAPTER 9

MASSACHUSETTS

Congamond Lakes — East Brimfield Reservoir —
Mashpee and Wakeby Ponds — Lake Quinsigamond —
Webster Lake — Quabbin Reservoir —
other favorites by county.

Massachusetts bass fishermen are a proud bunch of people who work hard to promote the sport in their state. Being centrally located and more populated than its northern neighbors, Massachusetts receives heavy fishing pressure; but this does not alter the fact that excellent bass fishing exists in some beautiful and scenic areas there. The beautiful fall harvest time, when the many apple orchards are filled with heavy-hanging fruit trees and are visited by tourists in pursuit of the wondrous views that the fall foliage brings, also announces one of the best times for bass fishing here.

Massachusetts, so rich in history and tradition, offers the tourist-angler an unlimited list of attractions to satisfy his desires. From the kettle lakes of Cape Cod to the wilds of the Quabbin Reservoir in the west, Massachusetts is sure to please the vacationing bass angler.

Congamond Lakes

Located about a mile east of Route 202 in Southwick, the Congamond Lakes consist of three basins totaling 465 acres: North Pond, 46 acres; Middle Pond, 277 acres; and South Pond, 142 acres. The clear and deep (40 feet) north basin is good trout water. The middle and southern basins are muddier, with areas of gravel and some areas of weeds. The lakes are heavily developed and have recreational use in the summer. There are two boat launchings, both located on the middle basin, one off Route 168 and the other off Point Grove Road to the north.

In spite of heavy fishing pressure, largemouth bass fishing is exceptional and Congamond is a favorite lake for bass tournaments. In summer, early morning and late afternoon fishing is productive; fall fishing for largemouth, after the fishing pressure decreases, is also rewarding. Spinners and jellyworms dropped into some of the deeper holes in the middle basin in

83

Try a dark curly-tailed rubber worm in the shallows of Webster Lake.

summer, or tossed into the shoreline in the fall, can produce some pleasant surprises.

The Springfield area offers all the necessary services to make your fishing trip to the Congamond Lakes pleasant.

East Brimfield Reservoir

The East Brimfield Reservoir was created by the U.S. Army Corps of Engineers in 1960 by damming the Quinnebaug River in Sturbridge. It is primarily a flood control project, in conjunction with the Thames River Basin Flood Control Program, but a great deal of attention was given to creating a recreational area for the public and, as such, it is a successful tribute to what fine planning with conservation in mind can do. The reservoir contains 420 acres, with a maximum depth of 22 feet. The bottom is rather weedy, and most of the shoreline is heavily wooded.

Access to the reservoir is along Route 20; boat launching facilities are also found along this road. Parking is more than adequate.

In order to boat from the northern section of the reservoir to the southern section, you must pass through a large culvert under Route 20. This is another favorite spot for bass tournaments, and the bass fishing is excellent for largemouth. The old submerged river bed which runs through the southern section of the reservoir is the place to fish for largemouth; spinner and buzz baits and rubber weighted weedless worms will likely pull in your limit in no time.

The town of Sturbridge is loaded with tourist services, including excellent lodging and a fine campground, because of the famed Old Sturbridge Village Museum located there. Antiques and good old Yankee food specialties are waiting for your enjoyment around every corner to make those off fishing hours more bearable.

Mashpee and Wakeby ponds

Located on picturesque Cape Cod, Mashpee and Wakeby ponds are really one pond split by a narrow strait of water. Located off Route 28 on Route 30 in the towns of Mashpee and Sandwich, Mashpee and Wakeby ponds total 729 acres of excellent bass fishing water. This is a coldwater pond, with an average depth of 28 feet and a maximum depth of 87 feet. The water is extremely clear; in summer the oxygen levels are adequate down to the 35-foot depth. The 7.3 miles of shoreline are about 40 percent developed. Sea run alewives provide good forage fish, and the smallmouth fishery here is noted for being healthy and scrappy.

The Mashpee River outlet is an exceptional trout stream; the area of the pond surrounding the river is a good place to try for bass, as are the several small islands in the northern pond.

There is a paved boat ramp and large parking area off Route 30, and numerous facilities for lodging and other necessities in the area.

This is another favorite site for bass tournaments, and because of its location on Cape Cod, a vacationer's paradise, it offers no end of possibilities for an extended vacation.

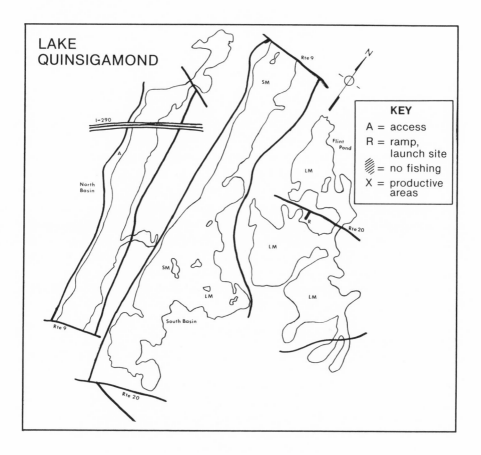

Lake Quinsigamond

Lake Quinsigamond is a good example of what can be done with a city lake to provide good recreational facilities for all, including the bass fisherman. Located between the city of Worcester and the town of Shrewsbury, this 722-acre lake is heavily developed with homes and commercial establishments, two state parks, several private beaches and marinas; it abounds with facilities for fishing, boating, water skiing, and other water sports.

The size of the lake allows fishing in relatively quiet sections of the lake away from the hustle and bustle of other activities. The shallow southern basin known as Flint Pond is the place to look for largemouth bass; the southern half of the basin above Flint Pond and north to the Route 9 bridge is a good area to try for smallmouth bass.

Rubber worms seem to be the largemouth bait of choice for use in the Flint Pond area, or small spinners when looking for smallmouth.

There is public access along Route 20, as well as at commercial marinas around the lake.

Webster Lake

From Worcester, drive west on I-290, then down Route 52 to Exit 1 to the Memorial Beach boat launching facility on Webster Lake. The 1270-acre lake is one of the best bass lakes in Massachusetts, despite some pretty heavy development along its shoreline. The water is clear, and the bottom is muddy and rocky; weedy areas can be found in the shallower coves.

Bass in Webster are hard-hitting and super fighters, in the shallows as well as in deeper water. We find rubber worms to be the best producers of large bass; some we have taken weighed over eight pounds.

An ordinary rubber eel won Carl Apperson the lunker bass trophy on this lake. Dark colored curly-tailed rubber worms, Rapalas twitched along shorelines in the early morning and late afternoon, and streamers trolled along the lake are all techniques sure to bring success here.

Webster Lake Marina offers access to the lake, as well as service for any of your boating and fishing needs.

Quabbin Reservoir

Quabbin Reservoir is the largest tract of wildland in Massachusetts. The reservoir is 25,000 acres in area, with a maximum depth of 180 feet. Route 2 cuts across the northern tip of Quabbin, Route 202 parallels the west side, and Route 9 skirts the south and runs into Route 32 and Route 202. This provides a good system of roads for easy access to the reservoir.

Created in 1937 by damming the Swift River, Quabbin has produced some monster bass in the past, but is now in trouble due to acid rain pollution. The Quabbin is the site of an eagle restoration project, and is also the location of a project to improve nesting conditions for the common loon.

But acid rain threatens this beautifully wild and windy reservoir. Recent experimentation by the Division of Fisheries and Wildlife, in which fish that were placed at the mouths of streams feeding the Quabbin on the western side died from the effects of acidification, forebodes a future that is less than bright for this great body of water. Efforts are underway to try and solve this problem and save the fisheries of the Quabbin, but the problem of acid rain is a large and complicated one.

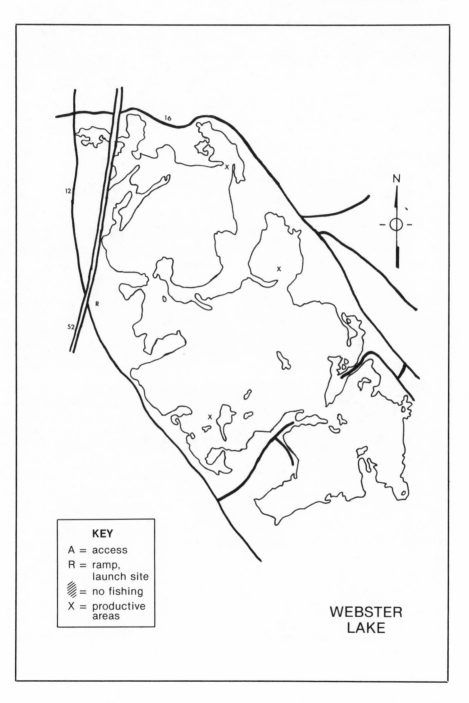

KEY

A = access
R = ramp,
    launch site
▨ = no fishing
X = productive
    areas

WEBSTER
LAKE

The whole family will enjoy fishing the structure on the Nashua River.

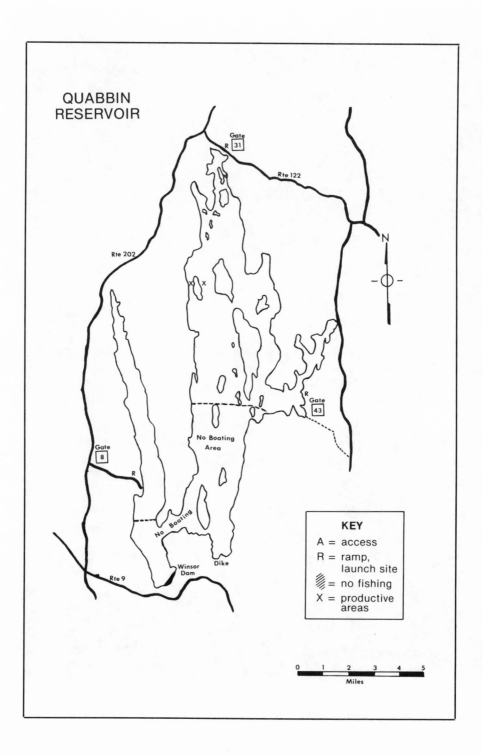

QUABBIN
RESERVOIR

Gate
R 31

Rte 122

Rte 202

N

X

R Gate
43

No Boating
Area

Gate
8

R

No Boating

Dike

Winsor
Dam

Rte 9

KEY

A = access
R = ramp,
launch site
= no fishing
X = productive
areas

0 1 2 3 4 5
Miles

Up to now, the bass fishing has remained good on the reservoir; with the help of concerned anglers, perhaps it will continue to be.

There are three boat ramps operated by the Metropolitan District Commission (at Gates 8, 31, and 43) with rental boats available. There are special regulations regarding the size and type of craft, and type of motor, allowed on the reservoir; information regarding these regulations and the fishing areas of the Quabbin can be obtained by writing to the Superintendent of the Quabbin Section of the Water Division at the Administration Building in Belchertown, or the office of the Water Division at 20 Somerset St. in Boston.

There is an area where no fishing is allowed around the Windsor Dam and the dike area of the reservoir, but the best largemouth fishing is in the area of Russ Mountain and in the shallows around Gate 33.

Deep runners and spinners are lures we have had the best success with here. Be careful of the famed afternoon winds on the reservoir. When the winds come up, around two o'clock every afternoon, the reservoir can become treacherous.

Wachusett Reservoir

Although no boats are allowed on Wachusett Reservoir, the months of May through mid-June produce some fantastic smallmouth bass. Fly fishing for smallmouth, as well as largemouth that are present, can be one of the most entertaining ways to enjoy this reservoir.

Located in the towns of West Boylston, Boylston, Clinton, and Sterling, the Wachusett sprawls over 8.4 miles, covers 4,135 acres, and boasts 37 miles of shoreline. The area immediately around the Clinton dam, a "no-shore-fishing" area, is the deepest part of the reservoir (129 feet), but the reservoir's average depth is 45 feet.

The Quinnapoxet and Stillwater rivers dump water into the reservoir all year, and the Quabbin Reservoir is another major source of water to the reservoir (via an underground aqueduct).

Entrances to the fishing areas are by foot only, and are from Route 70 by Gates 3 to 16, from Route 140 from Gates 17 to 27, and from Route 110 from Gates 28 to 37.

The large size of the smallmouth in Wachusett makes a visit to this reservoir a must, even though limited to shore fishing.

Connecticut River

One of the best bass rivers in Massachusetts is the Connecticut River which flows 70 miles through the state from north to south. The depth ranges from two to five feet in the backwaters to 40 feet in some of the cutouts on the fast currents and ebbs. This river, threatened by pollution in years past, now supports all types of fish.

The Connecticut is paralleled by Route 91 and crossed by Routes 202, 9, 2, and 90. There are launch areas from Turner's Falls, Greenfield, Old Mill, Holyoke, and Northampton. All are state ramps. These areas are where you will find the best bass fishing. This fine old lady of a river produces great in spring, fair in summer, and super in fall.

The Connecticut is exceptionally good to the average fisherman and holds a wealth of experiences along its banks. It is like living 150 years ago in some areas, and in others it is like being in the heart of a large city.

Surface plugs and spinner baits will be your best weapons in your search of largemouth bass on the Connecticut River.

Other Bass Waters in Massachusetts

Of the many bass waters in Massachusetts, we have selected some of the best to include in this section. Any pertinent and noteworthy information about a body of water is listed. A water preceded by an asterisk is to be considered a best bet for bass.

WESTERN DISTRICT

*Cheshire Reservoir (Cheshire, Lanesboro): Route 8; 418 acres; 3 basins make up the reservoir — the southern basin is very shallow and full of weeds, the middle basin is deeper and less weedy but there is no good access here except off a causeway where a canoe is the best craft to use; the northern basin has been the target of an extensive weed control program and there is a dirt boat ramp at the northeast tip; the access is sometimes very limited but if you can get on this reservoir you are in for the treat of a lifetime; the largemouth in here are *lunkers;* with no exaggeration at all, the biggest bass in the state may be in this reservoir.

Goose Pond (Tyringham, Lee): out of Lee center on Goose Pond Road; 225 acres; 45 feet maximum; this is a crystal clear mountain lake; public access is by a tarred boat ramp on the western shore just north of the outlet; there are few aquatic plants and a rubble bottom; there is a good population of SMB here and LMB are present.

Laurel Lake (Lee, Lenox): Route 20; 170 acres; 50 feet maximum; in the heart of the Berkshires with a public access ramp and 60 parking spaces located off Route 20 in the southernmost cove; there are extensive weed flats; rubber worm territory for the enticing of the LMB that inhabit this lake; the SMB population is limited.

Onata Lake (Pittsfield): off Route 7 out of Pittsfield on Lakeway Drive; 617 acres; 64 feet maximum; heavy fishing pressure and recreational use but the lake is in very good condition with a city park located on the lake; an oiled boat ramp and parking lot is located on the southeast shore; dense aquatic vegetation up to the ten foot depth and mostly in the northern coves; the bass fishing is good and weedless lures the bait to try.

Plainfield Pond (Plainfield): Route 116; 57 acres; 9 feet maximum; located about three miles northwest of Plainfield Center this is a lightly developed, heavily wooded pond nearly surrounded by state forest; a gravel boat ramp is located at the southeast corner of the pond; the coves are heavily weeded and weed beds are scattered throughout the pond; occasionally a lunker LMB is taken here.

CONNECTICUT VALLEY DISTRICT

Hampton Ponds (Westfield): Route 202; 198 acres; 31 feet maximum; very clear with a sandy and gravelly bottom; heavily developed shoreline; a stone launch ramp is provided by Forest and Parks; though the LMB population is heavily fished, there are some good fish here.

*Lake Warner (Hadley): off Route 63; 68 acres, 10 feet maximum; heavily weeded with a mucky bottom; development is light; the bass population here is in good shape and promises even better fishing in years to come; because the lake is about half covered with weeds during summer the weedless rubber worm is the best bait to try.

Swift River: The Quabbin Reservoir was created by damming this river and the same good fishing can be found on the river.

Westfield River: The area of the Westfield from Westfield to where the river joins the Connecticut River is the best area for bassing; this river can be fished the same as the Connecticut.

NORTHEAST DISTRICT

*Baddacook Pond (Groton): Martins Pond Road; 76 acres; 45 feet maximum; there is a large swamp at the northeast end of the lake and a town water supply at the other end. Weed beds consisting of water lily and milfoil are located around most of the lake; tarred parking lot and boat ramp off Martins Pond Road; Baddacook is known for the lunker LMB taken out of her every season, but you have to work hard for them.

Forge Pond (Littleton, Westford): Route 225; 212 acres; 30 feet maximum; gravel bottom with some weeds in shallows and coves; there is a dirt road next to the railroad tracks that runs along the northeastern shore; we have caught bass from shore in a little weedy cove here and have had good luck catching SMB while trolling through the deeper sections of the pond; access is limited but the fishing is excellent.

Jamaica Pond (Boston): Routes 1, 3, 28, 138; 68 acres; 53 feet maximum; sand and muck bottom with submerged vegetation in the shallows; the shoreline is undeveloped and owned by the Boston Parks Commission; a permit to fish here can be obtained from The Boston Parks Commission at City Hall; private boats are not allowed but boats are rented at the pavillion on the east side of the pond off Jamaica Way where fishing equipment is also rented; LMB fishing is excellent.

*Knops Pond (Groton): Routes 119 and 25; 204 acres; 30 feet maximum; Knops Pond was formed by raising the water level in a mill pond until it flooded out two smaller ponds to form this one large pond; the water is clear and there is abundant weed growth; the shoreline is heavily developed except for some conservation land near the northeast shore; heavy recreational activity in summer means early a.m. and late p.m. fishing is your best bet; excellent LMB fishing to be had here.

Massapoag Pond (Lunenburg): Lancaster Avenue; 56 acres; 15 feet maximum; there is a boat launching site off Lancaster Avenue; a variety of weed growth offers plenty of cover to fish for LMB; use your weedless rubber worms and spinnerbaits in and around the weeds and race worms across the pads dropping them into open water and watch the bass jump.

SOUTHEAST DISTRICT

Billington Sea (Plymouth): Exit 6 off Route 44 to South Meadow Road then left on Norton Park Drive; 269 acres, 10 feet maximum ; dirt boat ramp on Norton Park Drive; good pond to fish very early in spring before weed cover gets too thick; sea run alewives offer excellent forage for the LMB here; LMB can be found in the shallows using chartreuse spinnerbaits and rubber worms; an occasional SMB can be found here, too.

*Cook Pond (Fall River): Laurel Street; 154 acres, 18 feet maximum; the bottom is mostly rubble with some rock and mud; there is an excellent paved boat ramp, fishing pier and parking for 50 cars located off Laurel Street and run by the Division of Fisheries and Wildlife; the number of LMB in Cook Pond is fantastic; this is one of the most fertile ponds in the state and supports good populations of bass; there is no excuse for coming home skunked from this pond.

*Lake Nippenicket (Bridgewater): ½ mile west of Route 24 on Route 104; 354 acres; 6 feet maximum; this is an extremely shallow and very weedy lake despite its sandy bottom; the water is murky and weeds are particularly heavy in the northern end of the lake; a paved boat ramp is located off Route 104 and a cartop launch site is located off Elm Street on the western shore; Nippenicket has lots of structure and lots of LMB; It is an excellent place to practice the art of weedless jellyworm fishing.

Lawrence Pond (Sandwich): 1.5 miles off the Mid-Cape Highway on Great Hill Road; 138 acres; 27 feet maximum; this is a clear pond with a mucky bottom and sandy shoreline; there is a dirt boat ramp off Great Hill Road to accommodate smaller boats; this is a fair SMB pond; no LMB are present as of the latest studies.

Long Pond (Lakeville): Route 140; 1,721 acres, 10 feet maximum; Long Pond is the largest natural body of water in the state; this lake has been reported to have excellent populations of both LMB and SMB but has not been as popular among fishermen as it should be; it has the reputation of being a hard lake to "read"; a boat ramp is located on Route 140.

Monponsett Lakes (Halifax): Route 58; 528 acres; 13 feet maximum; this lake is divided into two basins by Route 58; a clear lake with a sand and rubble bottom, Monponsett has a moderately developed shoreline with some weedy areas; the LMB in this pond are to be found in the eastern basin; those in the western basin are small in size; this pond is just beginning to experience the effects of acid rain and is slowly going downhill; this is too bad because Monponsett used to be an excellent bass water.

Norton Reservoir (Norton): Route 140; 529 acres, 10 feet maximum; murky water and small amounts of vegetation except on the shore of this impoundment; access for boats is located on the northeast end of the reservoir, where Route 140 bisects the southern end and near the outlet dam; there is a huge population of white perch here that compete with the game fish species but LMB of some considerable size have come out of here in the past; there has been talk of stocking tiger muskies here to help decrease the perch population.

*Snipatuit Pond (Rochester): 5 miles west of Route 28; 710 acres; 6 feet maximum; extremely shallow, murky water surrounded by wetlands with a muddy bottom; lots of weeds along the shoreline with some patches scattered throughout; there is a dirt boat ramp located off Neck Road on the eastern shore; there is an excellent LMB population here with some large individuals; as we have seen many times, the sea run alewife population, when present, provides an excellent forage food for fattening up old mossy back.

CENTRAL DISTRICT

Big Alum Pond (Sturbridge): off Route 148; 195 acres; 45 feet maximum; the water is very clear, the shoreline about 80 percent developed; there are some weedy areas and a paved public boat launch at the southern end of the lake; Big Alum is a popular trout pond but spring SMB fishing here is excellent; for some special fun try flyfishing for SMB using a bushy fly or some bright colored bugs.

*Buffumville Reservoir (Oxford, Charlton): Putnam Road bisects the reservoir; 451 acres; 17 feet maximum; murky water with weedy western shoreline; lots of stumps and dead trees (excellent LMB cover) on the eastern shore of the southern basin; boat launching at the northern end of the southern basin off Putnam Road; there is a large culvert most boats can travel through to get to the northern basin; the shoreline is not developed except for a public swimming area; LMB are abundant all over the reservoir but concentrate on the southern basin for a superb fishing trip.

*Demond Pond (Rutland): 1 mile south of Route 122A on Pleasant Street; 119 acres; 27 feet maximum; clear water with a muddy bottom and some rocky areas; a small amount of weed growth; boat access is off Pleasant Street near the dam and will accommodate only smaller boats; this pond has quite a good population of LMB in the two to five pound range; fish fallen trees and ledges and holes around boulders.

Fort Pond (Lancaster): just north of Route 2 at the Lunenburg Road exit; 76 acres; 45 feet maximum; heavily developed shoreline; some aquatic weeds; gravel boat ramp located off Fort Pond Road at the southeastern tip; there is a good population of LMB with a few large fish.

Lake Singletary (Millbury, Sutton): 2 miles southwest of Millbury Center; 330 acres; 37 feet maximum; public boat launching off West Main Road at northern end of the lake; both LMB and SMB are here and the fishing is good; fish submerged rocks or weedy bottomed areas; spinnerbaits are good here as well as medium runners.

*Chauncy Lake (Westboro): off Route 9 to Chauncy Street; 185 acres, 20 feet maximum; very lightly developed shoreline; Department of Fisheries and Wildlife launching ramp located off Chauncy Street; both LMB and SMB fishing is very good here with the LMB frequenting the weedier coves while the SMB can be found around submerged trees and rocks.

*Lake Denison (Winchendon): off Route 202; 85 acres; 15 feet maximum; part of the Birch Hill Flood Control Project, the lake remains undeveloped and there is a 10 h.p. limit on outboards; there are campgrounds located on the northern and eastern shores; there are some lily pads in the shallower areas; the latest fish surveys showed that this lake has a healthy population of LMB and if you work the weedy areas of Denison you will be sure to hook up with some.

*Long Pond (Rutland): Route 122; 186 acres; one of the better bass ponds in Massachusetts, Long Pond is really split into three ponds with the 81 acre southern pond having the best access located directly off the highway; the other two ponds are extremely weedy and shallow with limited access; the LMB are the most abundant fish here and will offer you many enjoyable hours of fishing; use your weedless rigs and play the cover.

*Manchaug Pond (Sutton-Douglas): Manchaug Road; 360 acres; 30 feet maximum; heavy development and recreational use does not seem to hamper the bass fishing here for which the lake is known; a large paved boat ramp is located on the northwest corner of the lake with parking for 50 cars; both the LMB and SMB fishing is best in the early a.m. and late p.m. due to the heavy traffic; fish the coves at the northern end of the lake, the western shoreline, and the shallows at the southern end.

Whalom Pond (Lunenburg, Leominster): off Route 13 at the rear of Whalom Amusement Park; 99 acres; 48 feet maximum; a paved ramp is located at the northeast corner of the lake; the closeness of this lake to urban areas causes heavy recreational use and at times the bottom of this lake is covered with debris; this is a good bass lake that is heavily fished and suffers from a common insect that thrives in urban areas — the litterbug.

Whitney Pond (Winchendon): Route 12; 110 acres; 31 feet maximum; weeds line the perimeter of the undeveloped shoreline; cartop boat launch via a gravel ramp is located off Central Street; some fairly good sized LMB exist in this pond; fish the edges of the weeds and cover.

TWO CLEANUP SUCCESS STORIES

The Nashua River

If a tangle with old mossy back is what you are after and you really do not care about the edibility of your catch then the Nashua River in Pepperell, Massachusetts is bass heaven. The reason we have chosen to include the Nashua in this book is because the river has been said to be one of the first "cleanup success stories." Up until the mid-1970s, this river was used as a garbage dump for paper mills and sewers and was famous for the shades of color that it would turn from day to day and the stench that fumed from its surface.

Through the efforts of concerned individuals and the Nashua River Watershed Association and cooperation from government, towns and industry this once beautiful river has been cleaned up and the present goal for the river is to make it fishable and swimmable.

At present the river is being enjoyed for recreational activities such as boating and canoeing. Fish and wildlife have returned in glorious numbers and the largemouth are huge and healthy.

The Massachusetts Division of Fisheries and Wildlife have found possible toxic concentrations of chromium and lead in some of the game fish taken here but the fish are healthy and growing. It is not known yet if the eating of these fish will cause health problems and so it has been suggested that it remain a fish-for-fun area. But if fun is what you are after then this is the place. Incredible fish are caught here all summer with some fish going in the ten pound range.

Access can be gained off Route 119 in Groton, Mass. Float down this river in a canoe and fish the backwaters, the many stump fields and where the trees overhang the water. Use blue, motor oil, and green rubber worms.

The Merrimack River

The Merrimack River used to be filled with nothing but suckers and eels. Industrial and municipal pollution had taken a heavy toll on this famous river but all that is in the past now and the 110-mile long Merrimack has become the local hotspot for all kinds of fishing, including the return of the Atlantic salmon which is reviving an interest among local fishermen and attracting vacationing fishermen as well.

Bass fishing on the Merrimack is great, especially in the area of Lawrence, Massachusetts. From the railway bridge just below Route 28 downstream fishing is excellent. There is no fishing above the bridge to the falls, about a 120-foot stretch of river.

It is hard to get a boat or canoe into the river until well into May because of high and treacherous water. When launching is feasible a ramp is located directly in front of a municipal parking lot on the north bank.

Fish the slower moving areas and the pools for great largemouth and smallmouth action. Bright and flashy spinners seem to work the best for us here. About mid-May you may even latch on to a small striper. Because of diminishing populations of stripers, Massachusetts has enacted a 24 inch minimum size limit on stripers and most of the ones caught are undersized, but they will give you a fight well worth the effort.

Later in the season when the water levels are lower the stretch of river from Lawrence to Haverhill has miles of wadable water. Largemouth can be caught in the small pools and at the edges of rapids where the oxygen supply is greatest.

Tackle and information on the Merrimack can be obtained at Al's Rod and Gun Shop, 400 Broadway, Lawrence, Ma. 01841. Telephone (617) 683-0310.

Morning on the reclaimed Nashua.

Maine offers miles of the rocky shoreline that smallmouths love.

CHAPTER **10**

MAINE

Sebago Lake — Little Sebago — Thompson Lake —
Moose Pond, Long Lake, Pleasant Lake — Belgrade
Lakes — Lake Massalonskee — Great Pond —
other favorites by county.

Slipping across the Piscataqua River, the eastern border of New Hampshire, we enter "Vacationland," the largest state in New England and the only one still boasting wilderness and unspoiled land areas of such vastness that one must actually hike or fly in to some areas to enjoy their secret beauty.

Maine, the borders of which contain 16,000,000 acres of woodland and 5,770 lakes and ponds of more than one acre, is rich in wildlife — and fishing waters.

Bass are not native to Maine, according to Regional Fisheries Biologist J. Dennis McNeish, and the two species were introduced into the state separately. The smallmouth were introduced in 1869 in waters such as Cochnewagon, Phillips, Newport, and Cobbosseecontee lakes.

Smallmouth, according to recent studies, have been found in 417 Maine lakes totaling 487,181 surface acres. The smallmouth of Maine support principal fisheries (those waters where they are abundant and contribute *significantly* to the angler's catch) in 372 of these lakes.

The largemouth bass was introduced to Maine waters in the late 1800s — the first recorded introduction was at Forbes Pond in Gouldsboro, Maine in 1897. Eventually successful establishment of populations in Great Pond and Messalonskee Lake, in the Belgrade Lakes region, came about. Largemouth are now found in 226 lakes totalling over 145,140 surface acres, with successfully established principal fisheries in 211 such lakes.

The best fishing for smallmouth is found in southern and eastern Maine, and more than 90 percent of the principal fishery for the largemouth is found in the southern part of the state. Maine's slow-moving rivers and streams also contain significant populations of both largemouth and smallmouth.

Angling pressure is low, and the populations of bass in Maine are sufficient to provide the quality bass fishing that dedicated bass anglers seek. Black bass is by far the most important of the warm water species in Maine. Coldwater species enthusiasts remain skeptical about the introduction of black bass to Maine waters, however, and much is being done to prevent undue pressure on coldwater species, and to educate anglers in the use of the bass fishery.

There has been a marked increase in the number of bass tournaments and clubs dedicated to black bass angling throughout the state of Maine, indicating the growing interest in the species. One of the largest of these clubs is the Pine Tree Basscasters, which sponsors bass tournaments across the state. For more information on Pine Tree get in touch with Jim Stewart, Box 59, West Kennebunk, Me. 04094, (207) 985-7547 — or Robert Lehioulliea, 292 West St., Biddeford, Me., 04005, (207) 499-2605.

We have spent certainly many pleasurable and productive angling hours on Maine lakes and rivers; here one can find sublime unspoiled beauty not to be reproduced anywhere else in New England. It has been a difficult task to pick the "best" bass waters in the state of Maine, for indeed there are a multitude of candidates; but we have done so, keeping in mind that, for most fishermen, accessibility is a prime consideration.

Sebago

The most obvious choice for the number one position is Sebago Lake in Cumberland County. This lake covers a massive 28,771 acres and is 316 feet deep at its center. The surface temperatures of the lake reach 78 degrees in mid-summer but, at the same time, may be only 41 degrees at 300 feet. A lake of this size and temperature contrast provides numerous hiding places for bass, as well as for the trout and salmon for which it is famous.

Sebago is located along Route 302 from outside Portland to North Windham, and north to South Casco along Route 35, then to Naples along the east side of the lake. Along the west side of the lake runs Route 114; along this route are many little coves where bass lurk continually.

Hotspots to try are in the area of Inner and Outer islands at the Muddy River and at the mouths of Batchelder and Nason brooks. You may launch a boat at the Nason Brook area for a fee. The shallows around the Northwest River also offer excellent largemouth fishing.

Sebago is just now coming into its own as far as bass are concerned. You may even run across a special treat — calico bass — for Sebago is home to this member of the bass family as well. We have found that Sebago has been producing more and more bass of considerable size early in the season. We believe that Sebago is going to be number one bass country in the near future — and, because of its accessibility and the number of accommodations and services available, it will likely become a prime target for weekend bass fishermen.

Sebago Marine, at the junction of Routes 11 and 114, offers services to meet any of your marine needs while visiting the lake, including boat rentals, tackle, and information.

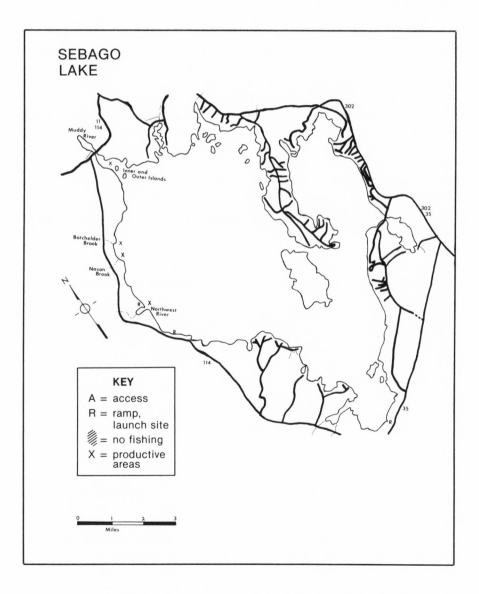

Small spinners and grubs are super baits to use in some of the shallows and backwaters of Sebago where depths are 25 feet or less. We have also had success trolling the edges of the lake in slightly deeper waters during the colder weather using spinners and live bait. During the spring of 1983, we encountered many fishermen whose success with the bass of Sebago had led them to believe that this was one of the best bass seasons yet on this, one of Maine's most famous lakes.

Lodging is to be found in abundance along Route 114. Sebago Lake Camps, located in North Sebago (207-787-3211), offer housekeeping cottages, most of them winterized, and all the services necessary for the fisherman's convenience, such as nonresident licenses, bait, boats and motors, canoes, moorings, and ice fishing camps.

Migis Lodge, located one-half mile west of Route 302, offers 29 units on Sebago Lake with boats, canoes, and motors for rent. They have a dock, and offer dining on the premises.

Campgrounds are in abundance in and around the Sebago area. The four listed below are recommended for the full services that they offer — water and electric, sewer, pumping and dumping stations, on-the-grounds stores, laundry, recreational halls, swimming, boating, fishing — and they all allow pets! They are:

The Colonial Mast Campground
Naples 04055
Tel. (207) 693-6652

Kokatosi Route 85 Campground
Raymond 04071
Tel. (207) 627-4642

The Point Sebago Outdoor Resort
Casco 04015
Tel. (207) 655-3821

Simpson's Sebago Lake Campground
Rd. #1, Box 516A
Sebago Lake 04075
Tel. (207) 787-3671 or,
in winter, (207) 642-3368

These campgrounds, and most others, are open from early spring to early fall; the actual opening dates, however, may vary due to the unpredictable Maine weather.

There are several other well-equipped campgrounds along this route, and numerous general stores — and no end of local fishermen who are glad to help, friendly, and willing to share their experiences on Sebago.

In addition to Sebago Lake itself, many of Sebago's tributaries offer excellent bass fishing. On the Crooked River in Casco (off Route 121) from Route 117 downstream to Route 11, there is no limit on bass (other areas of the Crooked are restricted to artificial lures or fly fishing only); the Songo River at Casco and South Casco (off Route 35), the Jordan River, and the Northwest River are excellent bass waters, also. The mouths of these rivers, and any other streams that enter Sebago, are super spots to hunt the black bass.

The season on Sebago Lake runs from April 1 (or ice-out) through September 30, and from January 1 to March 31, with the standard limits: five fish or 7½ pounds, minimum 10 inches in length.

Little Sebago Lake

It may be called "little" Sebago but it is a big bass producer! Located east of Sebago Lake, this 1,898-acre, fairly shallow lake has a 52-foot maximum depth, and is a fine spot for both largemouth and smallmouth fishing.

Take Route 35 out of Raymond and head south — or take 35 north out of Sebago Lake Township to North Windham, then Route 115, which passes to the southeast of Little Sebago. A boat launching is available just off Route 115 in an area called Shelldrake Cove.

From early May through June, fish for bass in the shallows with bucktail spinners. Later in the spring, the coves and rocky ledges will yield bass. At this time, the largemouth hole up in the narrows. In late summer, fish just after sun-up and just before dark in the shallows where the bass come in to feed.

Twin Brooks Camping Area is located on the north side of the lake. It is a small campground (only 25 sites), but offers all necessary facilities. For more information, write:

Twin Brooks Camping
Gray, ME 04039
Tel. (207) 428-3832

Thompson Lake

A short distance north from Sebago Lake along Route 121 is Thompson Lake. Located in the southern tip of Oxford County, 4,426-acre Thompson Lake offers the crystal clear water and rocky shorelines that tend to make bass spooky and super fighters. We have taken six-pound bass from Thompson recently, and it seems they are still growing.

The Maine state record smallmouth bass — an eight-pounder — was taken from Thompson Lake in 1970; today, the lake offers similar possibilities for those in search of trophy bass.

No motorboats are allowed in the Heath section of the lake — the south-ernmost part of the lake, separated from the main water by a causeway.

Thompson is a good lake to slip a canoe into early in the morning before the sun begins to warm the surface. A tour of the shallows, using long casts and light tackle, is apt to net you some pleasing results.

Fishing is great from June right through September; bass can be coaxed to the hook quite readily in the Bar section of the lake, at its northern tip, as well as in and around Black and Megguier islands in the lake's mid-section. There is a boat launch at the southern tip of the lake on the west side.

The town of Oxford, located at the nothern tip of Thompson Lake, will be the place to go for your necessities while visiting this lake. Muskegon Camping Area, Oxford 02470, Tel. (207) 539-9689, is located on nearby waters, and offers many conveniences.

Cabins are for rent on the lake, many privately owned, for various rates. Contacting the Oxford Chamber of Commerce in early spring will get you all the help you need in selecting a cabin for your fishing holiday.

Moose Pond, Long Lake, Pleasant Lake

The Bridgton area offers no end of possibilities for lodging, camping and services. Moose Pond, Pleasant Lake, and Long Lake, as well as Thompson and Sebago lakes, are all within a few minutes' drive from the Bridgton area. The famous Tarry-a-While Resort on Highland Lake offers Swiss hospitality — and swimming, boating, fishing, tennis, sailing, windsurfing, waterskiing, and a public golf course. For good food and warm hospitality while on your bass fishing trip, contact the Hans Jenni Family at Box H, Bridgton 04009, or call (207) 647-2522.

Another fabulous resort to check out on your trip is the Chute Resort Cottages, situated on Long Lake one mile north of Naples on Route 35. This resort offers cottages with private wharves and fireplaces. For more information, write Phil Chute, Box 127, Naples 04055, or call (207) 693-6425.

Meade's Housekeeping Cottages, located on the east shore of Highland Lake, offers fully-equipped, heated cottages, and also boasts three cottages located on an island 300 yards from the mainland. Contact Ruth and Harold Meade, Route 2, Box 82, Bridgton 04009, or call (207) 647-2262.

Among the many good camping facilities in this area are:

Lakeside Pines Campground
North Bridgton 04057
Tel. (207) 647-3935

Salmon Point Campground
Bridgton 04009
Tel. (207) 647-3678

Vicki-Lin Campground
Bridgton 04009
Tel. (207) 647-2630

Moose Pond, north of Route 302 out of Bridgton, is prime bass country. Both Upper and Lower Moose ponds are excellent and productive bass waters; the upper basin, north of Route 302, is nearly pure bass and pickerel water. Live bait and spinners seem to be the killers here. Rubber worms are also deadly in the coves and off the points from mid-May through June. Depths range from four or five feet in backwaters to more than 100 feet in the center.

Summer and fall seem to produce the greatest number of three- to five-pound bass, and the warmer weather will allow you to fish Moose Pond in comfort. State boat launching facilities are available on the lake off Route 302.

Not as heavily developed as other lakes in the area, Moose Pond's shore-line is, for the most part, wooded. This lake gave up the state's largemouth record in 1968, a lunker at 11 pounds 10 ounces, and promises to be a good place to try if bettering that record is on your mind.

Situated at the base of the Pleasant Mountain ski slopes, and on the shore of Moose Pond, is the Pleasant Mountain Inn. The inn offers year-round comfort in its motel and main lodge. There is excellent dining, a private beach, and boats available. For more information and to make reservations, write Ken and Peggy Miller, Moose Pond, Bridgton 04009, or call (207) 647-2431.

Long Lake, in Bridgton via Route 302, though somewhat heavily populated by resort users, still offers excellent fishing and remains on our list of suggested bass waters. Early morning fishing is the key here, mainly to avoid waterskiing and boating tourists. Off-season produces great results, with early spring and fall your best bets.

Campgrounds, other lodgings, food, and related services dot the eastern shoreline of Long Lake. State boat launching facilities are located along Route 37 in North Bridgton. The backwaters of Long Lake out of the Naples area will produce good fighting bass. Use light tackle, grubs, and live bait.

East of Route 121 out of Casco and Otisfield is Pleasant Lake. Sandwiched between Long Lake and Thompson Lake, this small pond offers some challenging bass fishing.

BELGRADE LAKES REGION

From Waterville and Oakland, we head west to the picturesque town of Belgrade Lakes, the centerpoint for a tour of the Belgrade Lakes Region. The Belgrade Lakes Region rivals the Sebago Lakes Region in the easy accessibility of a variety of bass waters famous for their fishability and productivity, not to mention a certain pervading wilderness-type charm. Certainly, the Belgrade Lakes area offers more remote and less pressured waters than does the Sebago Region, and is famous for the bass that are found in any of its waters.

Lake Messalonskee

Perhaps the best water to fish in all of the Belgrade region is Lake Messalonskee; in our opinion, the Abenakis Fishing Camps have an ideal location here for the bass fisherman. The camp is located on the mouth of the Belgrade Stream, with direct access to 3,510-acre Lake Messalonskee. This stream is the place to try from early May through June and July. From Wings Mills to the lake, both largemouth and smallmouth are in abundance. Fishing in and around the stumps in this area in a small boat or canoe produces excellent results. Rubber worms and hellgrammites, and grasshoppers in July are sure to bring in the limit here.

The southern end of Lake Messalonskee is one large marsh; racing rubber worms across the tops of the weeds and letting them drop slowly into the water is a technique worth trying here.

The Abenakis Camps have hot and cold spring water and boats and motors are available. For more information, contact Andy and Muriel Jancovic at Dept. MF, Belgrade 04917, or call (207) 495-2294.

There is also a public launch at Belgrade Stream on Route 27, and another along Route 23 on the eastern side of the lake.

Great Pond

Great Pond offers no end of opportunities for excellent bass fishing; it offers a public boat facility and marina in the village of Belgrade Lakes. The best fishing is in June and September, along the shallows.

The 8,239-acre lake is the largest of the Belgrade chain of lakes, with a maximum depth of 69 feet. Though Great Pond is a major tourist attraction, it still offers great bass fishing in the areas known as Abena Point, Long Point, Jamaica Point, and Snake Point. A few nice honey holes are hidden along the southeastern shore of Hoyt Island as well. Crankbaits and spinners are limit producers here.

Among the suggested accommodations are the following: Woodland Camps, located on the shores of Great Pond, have 16 log cabins and a main

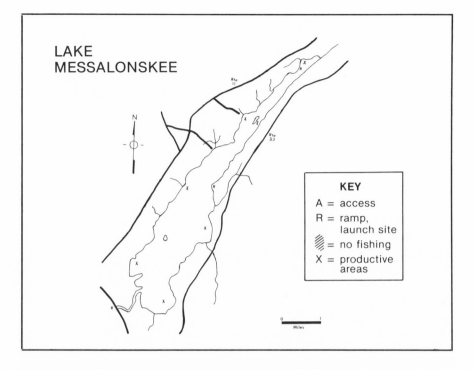

LAKE
MESSALONSKEE

KEY

A = access
R = ramp,
    launch site
= no fishing
X = productive
    areas

lodge and offer home cooking and a family atmosphere. They are open from mid-May to mid-September. Contact Betty Grant, Woodland Camps, P.O. Box 445, Belgrade Lakes 04918, or call (207) 495-3359 (495-2251 after May 15); Great Pond Motel and Wilderness Campground, located a short distance from the public boating facility and marina, are also open in the fall; boat rentals are available. Contact Mr. and Mrs. Stephen LaFreniere, Rte. 27, Belgrade Lakes 04918, or call (207) 495-3817; Deering's Snug Harbor Camps, situated on Great Pond, offer heated accommodations for from two to six people. The rates include all meals, and there is no charge for boats during May and June. Contact Mr. and Mrs. Llewellyn A. Ashland, RFD #1, Box 200, Belgrade 04917, or call (207) 465-3005 or 495-3445; Crystal Spring Camps offer waterfront cabins, dining, rates which include all meals, boats and motors, and guides to help you find the hot spots on Great Pond. They are open from June 18 to Sept. 3. Contact Harry and Patricia Gerrish, Box 125P, Hanover, Ma. 02339, or call (617) 826-2866 (after June 19, (207) 397-2542).

While in this region, we also suggest a stay at Bear Spring Camps, situated at the north end of Great Pond. Open from May through October, they offer 32 (two- to five-room) lakeshore cottages with open fireplaces, full baths, and heat. Their rates include all meals. Contact Bert Mosher, Oakland 04963.

East Pond

East Pond has been a superb smallmouth lake in recent years, and hosts both the bronzeback and its bucket-mouthed cousin in abundance.

June is the most productive month for bass fishing here. A free boat ramp is located at the northeast tip of the lake (also a good place to start fishing); also try the weedier area to the north and in and around Miller Islands.

Take Route 8 out of Augusta to East Pond's 1,705 acres of fun fishing.

Downeast Outfitters LTD is located here and will be able to meet any and all of your needs on your fishing trip to the Belgrade Lakes area, including meals, boats, cottages, and guides. Write P.O. Box 85, Oakland 04963, or call, from September to April, (603) 432-5371 and, from May to August, (207) 465-7473.

We suggest staying at either of the two following facilities: Rocky Shore Camps, open from June 20 to Labor Day, offer free boat and motor during June. They have lakefront cottages and dining. Contact Rocky Shore Camps, Box 3460, Oakland 04963, or call (207) 465-2203; Alden Camps offer cottages, boats and motors, and special June rates. Contact Alden Camps, Oakland 04963, or call (207) 465-7703.

North Pond

To the west of East Pond on Route 137 out of Smithfield is North Pond, possibly one of the best bass waters in the state. Both largemouth and smallmouth inhabit this 2,115-acre top producer.

North Pond is a shallow lake, with a maximum depth of 20 feet. Large areas of heavy weed beds make this a prime producer of largemouth, consistently weighing seven pounds or more. This is rubber worm territory!

A weedless rigged jellyworm tossed in the weeds and played slowly at the edges of cover will drive the bass crazy.

Pomleg Island, at the northern side of the lake, hosts bass on its southern shoreline and the shallow inlet to an area known as Little Pond holds bass at its edges.

Camps, a boat launch, and boat rentals are situated along Route 137. From ice-out in late April through the season, the fishing here is excellent.

Long Pond

Another Belgrade area lake that offers plenty of travelers' services, and fine largemouth and smallmouth fishing, is 2,714-acre Long Pond. Spread across the towns of Rome, Belgrade, and Mt. Vernon, Long Pond, though heavily developed as a tourist attraction, still offers scenic undeveloped areas of shoreline.

Long Pond is split into two lakes by a road crossing the narrow mid-section. The lower lake is best for largemouth. Fishing the weed beds in the shallows of this part of Long Pond will produce a good string of keepers. Carl Apperson's special techniques of racing a weedless rigged jellyworm across the top of the weeds and dropping it into open pockets of water will work wonders here later in the season when the weeds are thick.

Smallmouth inhabit the rocky shoreline of the upper part of Long Pond. Live bait, worms and shiners, will bring in a nice string.

Boat launching is available along Route 27, which passes parallel to the eastern shoreline, as well as along the road across the lake's mid-section and at the dam at Belgrade Stream.

Parker Pond

Crayfish or crayfish artificials are the baits of choice for Parker Pond, located off Route 41 out of West Mount Vernon. The 1,610-acre lake has a rocky bottom and is dotted with islands in its northern reaches. Both large-mouth and smallmouth fishing are excellent; the bass taken here are often "lunker" size. The fishing is best from spawning early in June through July. The depths range from shallows on the western shore (4-11 feet) to 76 feet at the center.

The boat launching off Route 134 will accept small boats; larger boats have also been launched. This is a great lake to visit while staying in the Great Pond/Long Pond area.

Webber Pond

Webber Pond in Vassalboro gives up trophy-sized smallmouths every season, and is one of the better largemouth waters in the area. The northern half of the lake is fairly shallow and becomes covered with algae bloom during the summer, but a weedless rigged jellyworm will work miracles.

Areas to try first are Clark Brook, Town Farm Island, Church Island, and Marriner's Point, as well as the Seven-Mile Brook outlet to the Kennebec River.

There is a boat launching at Seven-Mile Brook, and all other facilities and services are available in the area.

Lake Cobbosseecontee

A tour of Maine's best bass fishing spots cannot fail to include Lake Cobbosseecontee. This lake has long been considered one of the best bass waters in the Northeast.

From mid to late April through early May and on into June, this 4,950-acre bass heaven will net you some fine specimens.

At dawn and dusk, the bait fish school heavily on Lake Cobbosseecontee, making for excellent top-water fishing. Bright-colored poppers and a variety of colored spinner baits aimed at the edges of weed beds in the extensive swampy areas will always pay off.

The shallows around Farr's Cove and at the Cobbosseecontee Stream outlet are good bets to explore while wandering the lake in pursuit of ole mossyback.

In summer, drop-off areas and deeper water around the islands, fished with deep-running crankbaits, produce excellent results.

Boat ramps are available on Route 135 in East Monmouth and just north of Cobbosseecontee Stream on the opposite side of the lake.

Lakeside Haven in Winthrop offers boats, motors, canoes, and an excellent guide service. They have cabins and housekeeping cottages on the lake. For more information, contact Lakeside Haven, Route 202, Winthrop 04364, or call (207) 395-4466; or contact Stan and Shirley Amidon at their winter address: 309 3rd Isle So., Bayonet Point, Fl. 33567, telephone (813) 868-6878.

Birchwood Housekeeping Cottages, situated on Lake Cobbosseecontee, offers 16 fully equipped cabins of from one to five rooms. Boats and motors are for rent. Contact 20M Estaugh Ave., Hadonfield, NJ 08033; after May 15, Box 267M, E. Winthrop 04343.

Timber Trail Campground in Winthrop 04364 is another good bet for those who prefer camping. Call (207) 395-4376.

Damariscotta Lake

One of the best sources of smallmouth bass in Maine is this, the largest lake in Lincoln County. It is located in Jefferson, Nobleboro, and Newcastle; take Route 1 to Damariscotta, then Route 213 which parallels the western shore of the lake.

Damariscotta Lake is 4,625 acres BIG! — and contains every type of fishing habitat. The northernmost basin is deep and serves the landlocked salmon well. The southern basin leads to a dam with a fishway, where the largest alewife trapping operation in Maine attracts many sightseers.

The middle basin (1,544 acres) is bronzeback country, with superb fishing at the narrows between the upper and middle basins, and in an area midway along the western side of the basin, known as the Devil's Triangle. From ice-out through the season, and even in winter, Damariscotta Lake is a top-notch producer of bronzebacks.

Damariscotta Lake State Park is located on the northeast shore of the lake; private cottages line the upper shoreline.

Town Line Campsites offer 55 well-equipped sites in a good location. For more information, write Town Line Campsites, Nobleboro 04572, or call (207) 832-7055.

Boat launching facilities are available at the northernmost tip of Great Bay and at the southernmost tip (outlet) of the lake.

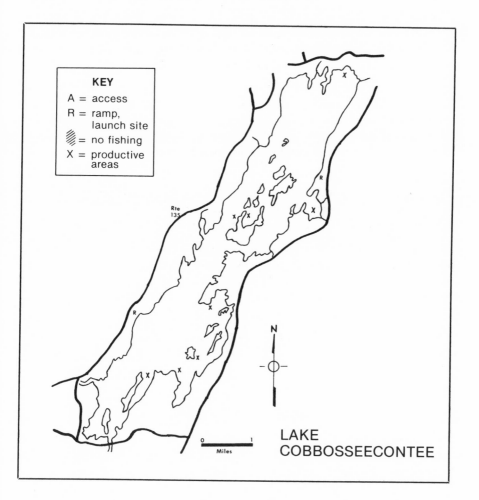

KEY

A = access
R = ramp, launch site
= no fishing
X = productive areas

LAKE COBBOSSEECONTEE

Other Interesting Bass Waters in Maine

There are numerous lakes, ponds, and rivers in Maine that will provide many hours of productive bass fishing. The following list, by county, will provide you with some of the more interesting bass waters. (There are many more small ponds and rivers that contain bass but it would require a separate book to list them!) Some pertinent information, including the nearest towns and access routes, is given after each listing. The waters preceded by an asterisk are our suggested "best bets" for those seeking a run-in with the black bass.

ANDROSCOGGIN COUNTY

*Androscoggin Lake (Leeds, Wayne): Route 106; 3,826 acres; 38 feet maximum; June, July, and September; good LMB and SMB fishing particularly around weedy areas at Dead River outlet; campsites on Route 106; boat launches on Route 106 and in Wayne at northern tip of lake.

Auburn Lake (Auburn): Route 4; 2,260 acres; 118 feet maximum; late April-June; SMB on live bait; fishing prohibited in area marked by buoys at pumping station.

AROOSTOOK COUNTY

East Grand Lake (Danforth, Weston, Orient): off Route 1; 16,070 acres; 128 feet maximum; mid-May through mid-June; this lake is on the international boundary between Maine and New Brunswick (special restrictions and limits apply); SMB; boat launching, campsites, and cottages available.

Molunkus Lake (Molunkus): Route 2 out of Macwahoc; 1,050 acres; 38 feet maximum; May through July; SMB; small boat and canoe launch at Baker Brook on southern shore; Deer Run Sporting Camps, E. McGovern, P.O. Kingman, Me. 04451 offers cabins, boats, motors, canoes, guides; call (207) 765-3900, in winter, call (516) 423-5140.

Pleasant Pond (Island Falls): off Route 2; 1,832 acres; 63 feet maximum; mid-May through June; SMB; Birch Point Lodge offers guides, float planes, boat launch, campground and much more, write Island Falls, Me. 04747, telephone (207) 463-2515.

CUMBERLAND COUNTY

Adams Pond (Newfield): Junction Routes 110, 11.

Beaver Pond, Woods Pond (Bridgton): Route 302; use rubber worm weedless rigs in shallows.

*Coffee Pond (Casco): Route 107; no length limit on SMB; use bright colored poppers and spinners.

Dumpling Pond (Casco): Route 121; use small to medium spinners and rubber worms.

*Hancock Pond (Denmark, Sebago Lake): Route 107; 858 acres; 59 feet maximum; June through August; both LMB and SMB; boat launch at southwest shore.

Hatcase Pond (Dedham, Eddington): off Route 1A; 168 acres; 77 feet maximum; mid-spring; northern arm closed to fishing; SMB along rocky shoreline.

*Highland Lake (N. Bridgton): Route 302; mid-May through July; 1,401 acres; 50 feet maximum; cottages for rent all along lake; both LMB and SMB; use rubber worms with slip-sinker along bottom.

*Lakin Brook (Sebago): Route 107; fish deadwater areas with rubber worms.

Ledgemere Pond (Limerick, Waterboro): Route 5.

*Lower Kimball Pond (Fryeburg, Me., Chatham, NH): Route 113; limit five bass; no length or weight limit; see New Hampshire chapter.

*Otter Pond (Standish): late May through June; cannot be reached by car; use small spinners and small to medium roostertails.

*Range Ponds (Poland): Route 122; upper and middle ponds — 757 acres; 66 feet maximum; late April through season; great SMB fishing off rocky shoreline; small spinners work well; boat launches.

*Saco River (Porter, South Hiram, Kezar Falls, Cornish, East Baldwin, Steep Falls, East Limington, Bonny Eagle, West Buxton, Bar Mills, Salmon Falls, Saco, Biddeford): Large and diverse river — fish deadwaters, late May through June; state boat launching sites at Biddeford, Fryeburg, Brownfield.

FRANKLIN COUNTY

*Clearwater Pond (Farmington): Route 43; no limit; 751 acres; 129 feet maximum; SMB best in June along dropoffs and rocks; boat launch off Route 43.

*Webb Lake (Weld): Route 142; lakeside camping at Mt. Blue State Park; boat launching and rentals.

Wilson Pond (Wilton): Route 2; 480 acres, 88 feet maximum; SMB best in June; boat launch at mill in Wilton.

HANCOCK COUNTY

Branch Lake (Ellsworth): off Route 1A; 1,728 acres; 124 feet maximum; late April through May, June, September; SMB at southeastern tip, not far from boat launch.

Flanders Pond (Sullivan): Route 183; 537 acres; 32 feet maximum; spring; SMB around islands; small boat and canoe launch off Route 183 at southeastern tip.

Green Lake (Dedham, Ellsworth): Route 1A; 2,111 acres; 82 feet maximum; May and June; SMB; boat launches on every shore; heavy fishing pressure.

Jones Pond (Gouldsboro): Route 1; no limit.

*Long Pond (Mt. Desert Island): truly scenic and beautiful area with camping facilities on and off Acadia National Park; no limit.

Nicatous Lake (T3ND, T40MD, T41MD): dirt road access from Route 188 out of Burlington; undeveloped; 5,165 acres; 56 feet maximum; good SMB fishing from late April through June; boat launching.

Philips Lake (Dedham): Route 1A; no limit; 828 acres; 98 feet maximum; SMB in early spring — also good ice fishing; small boat and canoe launches off Route 1A at mid-lake on eastern shore.

Ripple Pond, Round Pond, Somes Pond (Mt. Desert): no limit; see Long Pond.

Toddy Pond (East Orland): Routes 1, 3; 1,978 acres; 122 feet maximum; May, June, September; SMB; boat launch at Route 176; all facilities and services.

KENNEBEC COUNTY

*China Lake (China, Vassalboro): Routes 9, 202; 3,832 acres; 85 feet maximum; mid-April through September; deep spring-fed lake; both LMB and SMB; shallows around Jones and Wards brooks in early spring, dropoffs around China Neck and Bradley Islands in summer; boat launch off Route 32.

*Cochnewagon Pond (Monmouth): Route 132; 385 acres; 28 feet maximum; both LMB and SMB; LMB excellent in October, will produce lunkers; use crankbaits and spinners along eastern and southern shoreline; boat ramp at Wilson Stream on Route 132.

Echo Lake (Fayette, Mt. Vernon, Readfield): Route 41 to West Mt. Vernon; 1,061 acres; 117 feet maximum; mid to late June best; both LMB and SMB; fish rocky inner shoreline for great SMB action; state boat launch.

Horseshoe Pond (West Gardiner): off Routes 9, 126.

*****Maranacook Lake** (Readfield, Winthrop): Route 41 out of Winthrop; 1,673 acres; 118 feet maximum; late April through June, September; shallows in northern arm of lake for LMB; drop-offs and islands for SMB; state boat launching off Route 41 at Dead Stream on northwestern tip of lake.

*****Salmon and McGrath Lakes** — "**Ellis Pond**" (Belgrade, Oakland): Routes 8, 137, and 11; combined acreage 1,040 acres; 57 feet maximum; May, June, and September, also good ice fishing; excellent LMB and SMB fishing in both lakes; try jellyworms or eels; boat launching and campsites on Route 137; boat launch on Route 8.

*****Threemile Pond** (Vassalboro, Windsor): Route 202; 1,077 acres; 37 feet maximum; SMB off rocky shore and dropoffs; LMB early a.m. and late p.m. in shallows; state boat launch off Route 202.

Torsey Pond (Mt. Vernon, Readfield): Route 41; 770 acres; 45 feet maximum; SMB; small boat and canoe launch.

KNOX COUNTY

Alford Lake (Hope): Route 105; no limit; state boat launching site.

Crystal Pond (Washington): Routes 105 and 220; no limit.

Washington Pond (Washington): Routes 105 and 220; no limit.

LINCOLN COUNTY

*****Biscay Pond** (Bremen, Bristol, Damariscotta): Route 130; 253 acres; 61 feet maximum; early April through May; good SMB fishing.

OXFORD COUNTY

*****Anasagunticook Lake** (Hartford): Route 140; no limit.

Granger Pond (Denmark): Route 160; no limit; nearly exclusively warmwater species.

Horseshoe Pond (Lovell): Route 5; no limit; no motorboats over six horsepower; good canoe area — small, but good results.

Keewaydin Lake (Stoneham): no limit.

*Kezar Lake (Lovell): Route 5; 2,510 acres; 155 feet maximum; use rubber worms, bright-colored poppers, and jigs; mid-May to June; both LMB and SMB; boat launch at the narrows on west shore.

Lovewell Pond (Fryeburg): Route 302; 1,065 acres; 45 feet maximum; SMB along dropoffs, May through July.

Sand Pond (Norway): Routes 117 and 118; no limit.

PENOBSCOT COUNTY

Hermon Pond (Hermon): Route 95, exit 43; 461 acres; 17 feet maximum; late spring-summer; fish Soudabscook Stream area for SMB; boat launch.

Junior Lake (Lakeville): off Route 6 out of Springfield; 3,866 acres; 70 feet maximum; remote lake — best access by boat up Junior Stream from West Grand Lake; SMB.

*Mattanawcook Pond (Lincoln): Route 6; 832 acres; 20 feet maximum; good-sized SMB are taken here each year; June through July; boat launching on western shore.

*Pushaw Lake (Hudson, Old Town, Orono, Glenburn): off Route 221 between Glenburn center and Hudson; 5,056 acres; 28 feet maximum; swampy and weedy shoreline, SMB fishing good; May through July; boat launching and campsites on eastern shore.

Wassookeag Lake (Dexter): Route 7; 1,062 acres; 86 feet maximum; good SMB country especially along western shoreline; late April through season; boat launch.

PISCATAQUIS COUNTY

First Buttermilk Pond (Bowerbank): off Routes 16, 6 out of Sebec; no limit; live fish used as bait prohibited.

*Sebec Lake (Dover-Foxcroft): Route 153; 6,800 acres of excellent SMB water; no limit; cabins on the lake; state boat launching facilities; suggested places to stay: Two Falls Housekeeping Cabins on Wilson River at the head of Sebec Lake, May through November, rental boats and motors; drive or fly in to private airstrip; write RFD #2, Box 178, Guilford 04443, or call (207) 997-3625;Law's Camps on the shore of Sebec Lake, boat provided, motors for rent, boat launching; write RFD #2, Box 54, Dover-Foxcroft 04426, or call (207) 564-3093; Peaks-Kenny State Park on Route 153 offers camping at Sebec Lake.

SAGADAHOC COUNTY

*Nequasset Pond (Woolwich): Route 1; 430 acres; 63 feet maximum; LMB and SMB around inlets and outlet — Nequasset Brook; May through June; boat launch.

SOMERSET COUNTY

Embden Pond (Embden): Route 16 out of North Anson; 1,568 acres; 158 feet maximum; fish dropoffs around northern and southern shoreline with deep runners for SMB.

Great Moose Lake (Hartland, Harmony): Route 151; 3,584 acres; 50 feet maximum; May through June; SMB; boat launch off Route 151.

WALDO COUNTY

Bowler Pond (Palermo): Route 3; no limit; opens last Saturday of April.

*Lake St. George (Liberty): Route 3; 1,017 acres; 65 feet maximum; late April through season; fish edges of spring feeders; boat launching, rentals, and camping at Lake St. George State Park off Route 3.

Pitcher Pond (Northport): Route 1; tourist facilities of all kinds in the area.

*Sheepscot Pond (Palermo): Route 3 passes north of lake; 1,215 acres; 132 feet maximum; no limit; gravel boat launching site run by Sheepscot Fish and Game Association on Route 3; good SMB fishing on rocky shoreline on east and north of lake.

WASHINGTON COUNTY

Big Lake (Indian, T27ED, T21): off Route 1 out of Princeton; 17,792 acres mostly undeveloped; May through August; SMB around the numerous islands; Lakeside Inn and Cabins, Box 36, Princeton 04668, or call (207) 796-2324.

*Cathance Lake (Cooper): Route 191; no limit; 2,905 acres; 75 feet maximum; late April through September; boat access at store on Route 191; SMB located mainly at eastern shores of Birch Point and at northeastern area of lake; Sunrise C. Canoe Expeditions located here, professional Maine guides; complete outfitting services, maps; write SCCE, Grove Post 04638, or call (207) 454-7708.

*Crawford Lake (Crawford): Route 9; 1,677 acres; 27 feet maximum; mid-May through June and September; boat launch off Route 9; this lake offers an interesting scenic tour worth the effort; by leaving Crawford via the Maine River, the northeast inlet to Crawford, you can travel up the Maine to the Mud Lakes and then on to Pocomoonshine Lake; SMB fishing is good all the way; development is light and the area is surrounded by woods; a true adventure in the wilds of Maine.

West Grand Lake and Grand Lake Stream (in the wilderness off Route 1): fly fishing only; April 1 through September 15; Leen's Lodge is reached by highway routes or amphibious plane from Bangor; write Leen's Lodge, at Grand Lake Stream 04637, or call (207) 796-5575; winter address Box 100, Brewer 04412, or call (207) 989-7363; great fishing in mid-May through June, in the early a.m. and late p.m. in July, and in September.

Meddybemps Lake (Meddybemps): Route 191; 6,765 acres; 38 feet maximum; very rocky with many islands; great SMB action June through September; boat launch on Route 191 at Denny's River.

Pleasant Lake (T7R2, T6R1): undeveloped; off Route 6 out of Topsfield; 1,574 acres, 92 feet maximum; good SMB; Maine Wilderness Canoe Basin Campground, Springfield 04487, or call (207) 989-3636, ext. 631; boat launching.

Pocomoonshine Lake (Princeton, Alexander): off Route 1 out of Princeton or off Route 9 out of Alexander; 2,464 acres; 40 feet maximum; very productive SMB lake; June, July, August; boat launch; Pocomoonshine Lake Lodges offer cabins, boats, motors, guides and licenses; write Box 1617, RR1, Alexander 04694, or call (207) 454-2310.

Scraggly Lake (T6R1, T5R1): off Route 6 out of Topsfield; access by boat from Junior Lake to the outlet of Scraggly Lake; 2,758 acres; 42 feet maximum; excellent SMB fishing worth the trouble of getting to this area; boat launching but few other services.

Third Machias Lake (T43MD, T42MD, T5ND): 2,778 acres; 35 feet maximum; make arrangements to visit through Colonial Sportsman's Lodge at Grand Lake Stream; SMB fishing excellent mid-May through August.

Wabassus Lake (T5ND, T6ND, T43MD): north of Third Machias Lake, off Route 1 out of Princeton; good bass fishing; scenic and remote.

YORK COUNTY

Province Lake (Parsonfield, Me.; Effingham, NH): Route 153.

Milton and Northeast Pond (Lebanon, Me.; Milton, NH): Route 16.

Horn Pond (Acton, Me.; Wakefield, NH): north of Route 109, south of Route 110, east of Route 11; state boat launching site.

Balch Pond (Newfield, N. Shapleigh, Me.; Wakefield, NH): east of Route 11, south of Route 110.

*Great East Lake (Acton, Me.; Wakefield, NH): north of Route 109, south of Route 110, east of Route 11; state boat launching site at state line at dam; 1,768 acres; 102 feet maximum; both LMB and SMB; best late April through late May; fish western arm along dropoffs.

Bunganut Pond (Lyman): Junction Routes 111 and 35.

Moussam Lake (Acton, Emery Mills, Shapleigh): Routes 109 and 11; no limit; 900 acres; 98 feet maximum; heavy seasonal traffic — before and after summer season best fishing; SMB; boat launch on Route 109.

*Little Ossipee Lake (Waterboro): Route 5; 564 acres; 74 feet maximum; no limit; mid-May through August; northwest arm for good SMB fishing; use rubber worms; state boat launching site.

Square Pond (Acton, Shapleigh): east of Route 11, south of Route 110, north of Route 109; no limit.

Swan Pond (Lyman): Junction Routes 111 and 35; no limit.

*Wadley Pond (Lyman): Junction Routes 111 and 35; no limits; early May through June.

For more information on state parks in Maine, write: Maine Department of Conservation, Bureau of Parks and Recreation, State House Station #19, Augusta, Maine 04333. For information on licensing and regulations, write: Maine Department of Inland Fisheries and Wildlife, Information and Education Division, 284 State Street, Station #41, Augusta, Maine 04333; or call (207) 289-2871.

Fishing the shoreline at Pawtuckaway State Park.

CHAPTER **11**

NEW HAMPSHIRE

The Kingston area — Baboosic Lake — Arlington Mills Reservoir — Goose Pond — Pawtuckaway Lake — Wickwas Lake — Connecticut River — other favorites by county.

Blessed with a whole range of different types of fishing waters, from deep cold lakes to warm shallow ponds, New Hampshire is an excellent location to test your bassing abilities. Of the more than 1,300 lakes and ponds and 1,500 miles of streams in New Hampshire, the best of these, when it comes to bass fishing, are located from the Lake Winnipesaukee region south to the Massachusetts border.

New Hampshire is well noted for excellent smallmouth fisheries. In the late 1970s, however, it was noted by fishermen in this state that the smallmouth fisheries were declining, and that fishing for this species was becoming increasingly difficult in New Hampshire's larger waters, such as Squam, Sunapee, and Wentworth lakes.

The New Hampshire Fish and Game Department began a series of smallmouth bass investigations to determine the cause of this decline. It was noted in the larger lakes that there had indeed been a decline in certain year-classes, possibly due to certain fluctuating factors such as temperature, water levels, wind, and predators.

It was determined that these poorly-represented year-classes had been responsible for the decrease in the productivity of the smallmouth bass, but that this was probably temporary; there were strong hopes that the bass fishing would improve as soon as the stronger year-classes matured.

From all accounts, this has happened. You can expect to find a good share of smallmouth waiting for you in New Hampshire, particularly if you know where to look for them. Largemouth fisheries abound in New Hampshire as well, especially in the southeastern area of the state.

The Kingston Area — "Bass Heaven"

Nestled in the Kingston area of Rockingham County is a small "lakes region" that is bound to please any bass fisherman. Four lakes — Country Pond, Powwow River Pond, Kingston Lake (Great Pond), and Greenwood Lake — and the Powwow River, all accessible from Route 125, offer exceptional warmwater fisheries.

Country Pond's 255 acres are shallow, (maximum 30 feet) and very weedy, with a muddy bottom. Largemouth bass lurk all over this body of water, and the pond has an excellent reputation for good-fighting heavy-bodied bass. Almost half of this lake is swamp, so this is weedless rigged rubber worm territory. Other weedless rigged lures such as the frog, eels, and so on, will work well here.

Mid-May through June and again in September are the best times to fish open water. Country Pond is also ice-fishing heaven and is a mecca for the sport.

The Powwow River outlet of the lake is one area where the bass just wait their turn to jump on your hook. In fact, the entire Powwow River is excellent bass country and should be explored. There are three boat launching sites on Country Pond and an excellent campground, Country Shore Camping Area, right on the shores of the lake. The camping area offers 100 tent and trailer sites, all with electric and water and some with sewer hookups. The campground also offers mosquito control for your comfort. For more information write: Joe Boswell, P.O. Box 79, Plaistow, NH 03865 or call (603) 382-8659 in the off season or 642-5072 in season.

Following the Powwow River north, we find that it is the outlet for another great bass pond, Kingston Lake (sometimes called Great Pond). This 204-acre lake is the home of Kingston State Park, which offers public facilities and swimming.

Kingston Lake is less weedy and somewhat deeper than Country Pond (44 feet maximum), but offers comparably exceptional bass fishing. Route 11 runs along the eastern shoreline and there is a free boat launching site at the Powwow River outlet. Bass fishing is fast and furious all season, particularly around the shoreline of a large island in the middle of the lake. The area where Little River enters the lake on the northwestern corner of the lake is also good fishing.

Powwow River Pond between Country and Kingston lakes, and Greenwood Lake to the north, are all connected by the river systems in the area — all offer exceptional bass fishing.

This little territory, nestled between Routes 125 and 108, has got to be explored by any self-respecting bassman, and promises a fishing vacation filled with fish stories grandchildren love to hear.

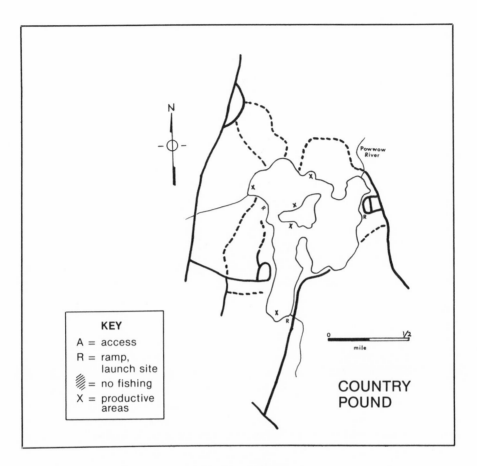

KEY

A = access
R = ramp,
    launch site
▨ = no fishing
X = productive
    areas

COUNTRY
POUND

Lake Massabesic

The site of many bass tournaments, Lake Massabesic is located in Manchester, and is part of that city's water supply. The 2,512-acre lake is clear and clean, and the shoreline is surprisingly undeveloped despite the lake's proximity to the largest city in New Hampshire.

Massabesic has a reputation across central New England for being a leading bass lake. The shoreline and bottom are rocky, perfect habitat for the smallmouth. Some weedier and shallow areas along Route 121 on the north side of the lake are home to the largemouth, as well as a narrow area in the middle of the lake called Deer Neck. The mouths of the various brooks feeding the lake are also excellent hiding places for the largemouth.

In early spring and throughout the summer, the fishing is good, and the fishing pressure is generally light. There is a boat launch at the traffic circle where Routes 121 and 28 intersect and several more launch sites around the lake.

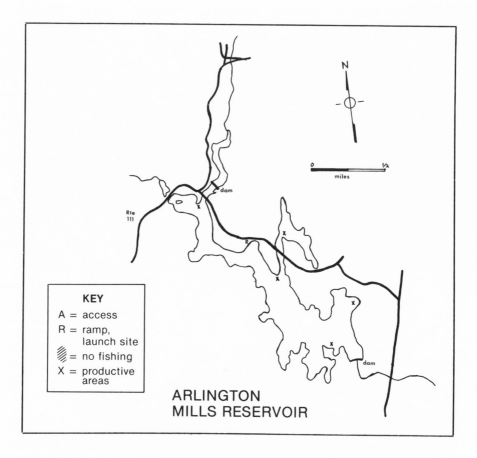

KEY

A = access
R = ramp, launch site
▧ = no fishing
X = productive areas

ARLINGTON
MILLS RESERVOIR

Arlington Mills Reservoir

Arlington Mills offers a challenge to the structure fisherman. When the reservoir was created, many stone walls, a couple of old mills, some cars, and various other structures were left on the bottom. These create unusual underwater structures to fish — any or all of them may be the home of old bucketmouth.

This 266-acre water is quite busy during the summer months because of its location in Salem, NH on Route 111. The best bass fishing will be in the early morning and the late afternoon — less traffic! The area just above the dam off Route 111, about 20 feet deep, is a good place to start fishing. Another good bet is the area around Wheeler Dam at the opposite end of the lake.

Fish the structures! Use weighted rubber worms — and explore! Best fishing begins in May and lasts until fall when the water in Arlington Mills is drawn down. A boat launching site is available about mid-lake on the north side off Route 111.

Baboosic Lake

Located in Amherst, NH off Route 101, Baboosic Lake has had rave reviews in the recent past. Several bass tournaments have been held on this 222-acre lake, which has a 29 feet maximum depth.

Although smallmouth bass have been stocked in Baboosic since 1983, they have failed to establish themselves. In 1955, undesirable species were reduced and largemouth bass were stocked — they have adapted well.

Baboosic offers varied fishing conditions — some areas are rocky and sandy, others swampy and weedy.

Fish the weedy areas on the western side of the lake in spring and summer in the early morning and late afternoon when the bass are feeding.

A boat launching site is located on the western shore.

Goose Pond

The state smallmouth bass record, a 7-pound 14½-ounce, 23¼-inch lunker, was taken from Goose Pond in 1970 by Francis H. Lord. Goose Pond has had a reputation for producing large bass ever since. Off Route 4 out of West Canaan, a local road leads out to Goose Pond and parallels the eastern shoreline. This 544-acre lake extends from a dam at Goose Pond Brook outlet to Marshall Brook inlet at the northern tip. Though the maximum depth is 30 feet in the middle, the average depth is around 12 to 15 feet, with some sharp dropoffs near the shore. The bottom is rocky, and there is an area of some weeds on the western shoreline, about mid-lake. Fish here for some exceptionally fine largemouth action. The rocky dropoffs are your best bets for king-sized smallmouth.

There is a free unpaved boat launching site on the eastern shore.

Pawtuckaway Lake

Home of the Granite State Open Bassmasters tournament, Pawtuckaway Lake has got to be one of the most important bass waters in New Hampshire. Its 903 acres offer a variety of conditions, from weedy areas and shallows to rocky shoreline and steep dropoffs.

Pawtuckaway State Park is a fantastic area to camp. Three-and-a-half miles north of the junction of Routes 101 and 156 in Nottingham, Pawtuckaway has 170 tent sites, a naturalist program, and all the necessary facilities. For more information on the park, call (603) 895-3031.

Fishing is excellent from mid-April through the season, particularly in the early morning and evening. Try the shallows in Neals Cove and the shoreline around Horse Island to the south, and Fundy Cove to the north, for largemouth action. Three state-owned boat launching sites are located on the lake.

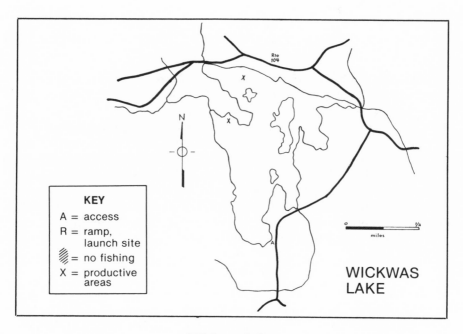

KEY
A = access
R = ramp, launch site
▨ = no fishing
X = productive areas

WICKWAS LAKE

Wickwas Lake

On Route 104 in Meredith, 328-acre Wickwas Lake is full of bucket-mouths and bronzebacks. Because of its proximity to Winnipesaukee and Winnisquam lakes, Wickwas is sometimes overlooked — but the bass are there, and it's well worth your time to give Wickwas a try.

In early spring, smallmouth will eat up spinner baits; largemouth will go after them, too, if you toss your lure along the shallower shoreline on the western side of the lake. From June through September, when a weedier growth lines the shore, change to jellyworms for super fights with lunker bass.

There is a boat launch on the southeastern shore and plenty of services available throughout the Lakes Region resort areas.

Connecticut River

We have gone into greater detail on the Connecticut River in the chapter on Vermont; certainly the information listed there holds true for New Hampshire. The Connecticut is the most important bass river in New England. From Hanover, New Hampshire south to Hinsdale, the lower half of the river is warmer and slow-moving and the best area for largemouth. Route 12 follows the river from Hanover to Westmoreland, and Routes 63 and 119 follow it from there to the Massachusetts border. The areas of the river that join the Mascoma, Sugar, Cold, and Ashuelot rivers are especially good places to explore for bass.

Lake Monomonac

Perhaps one of the best bass waters for both species is Lake Monomonac, located off Routes 202 and 119, just south of Cathedral of the Pines in Rindge, New Hampshire.

There is no closed season on this lake, and the limit is five fish with no weight or size restrictions (as of Jan. 1, 1980). Valley Marina, located on the New Hampshire side of the lake on Route 202, has a boat launching facility, tackle, rentals, and all the information you will need.

From the boat launching at Valley Marina you can start fishing right away. The water is four to 15 feet deep, with an excess of aquatic weeds and cover. On the right are lily pads and water hyacinth flats — about 60 acres of them! This is the area where we have taken our limit many days, and in many tournaments. The largemouth can reach weights in excess of 10 pounds in this lake because of the warm water and abundance of food.

Monomonac is fair in spring, but in early summer and mid-fall, she gives up her best in super-sized bass.

We have rated Monomonac one of the best bass fishing waters in New Hampshire because of its location in central New England, its full range of fishing conditions, and the abundance of both species found there.

It is not all heaven on this lake, though. She can get nasty very quickly. We have been caught in thunderstorms too far out to get to safety, and we had to wait out a downpour that looked like a wall of water about to claim us all. The weather is one thing you must keep an eye on all the time.

Fishing Monomonac is relatively simple. Mann jellyworms or spinner baits are the most productive. Again we must stress — use the lures you trust. They will not disappoint you here.

Lodging and dining facilities are limited, but can be found a short drive south into either Winchendon or Fitchburg, Massachusetts or north toward Jaffrey. There is a small campground in Monadnock State Forest, located four miles northwest of Jaffrey, New Hampshire off Route 124. Because of the lake's central location, you should be able to reach it from wherever you are staying in central New England, in most cases, in less than an hour's drive.

Lake Winnipesaukee

Lodging, dining, and camping facilities abound at Lake Winnipesaukee in central New Hampshire. The largest lake in New Hampshire, 28 miles long and 12 miles wide, Winnipesaukee is dotted with 274 islands ranging in size up to 1,000 acres. It contains 72 square miles of water and has 283 miles of shoreline; 170 feet is the maximum depth.

The lake is noted for smallmouth, but there are largemouth here, too. Winnipesaukee's sister lake, Winnisquam, located on the opposite side of Laconia, is the place to go if largemouth is your preference.

Located at Laconia, the headquarters of the White Mountain National Forest, Winnipesaukee sprawls over a large chunk of Belknap and Carroll counties. Within the national forest, facilities for camping, fishing, boating, etc. can be found everywhere. For more information on the offerings of the national forest, write to Forest Service, U.S. Department of Agriculture, Laconia, NH 03246.

Getting back to the lake itself, the best fishing is to be found on the eastern side of the central islands, and along the inlets of the great number of streams on the eastern side of the lake. Smallmouth will make up most of your catch; they seem to prefer live crayfish or crayfish simulated artificials. It has been our experience that the jellyworm performs exceptionally well also, when trolled along these areas. The bass fishing is extremely good from May through June.

Marinas abound in Laconia and Weir's Beach, as well as other points along the lakeshore. They are too numerous to mention here, but most all of them offer excellent facilities.

One of the nicer places to stay on the lake is the Silver Sands Motel and Marina located in Gilford, New Hampshire on Route 11B, three miles south of Weir's Beach. The motel and marina have two launching ramps, boat slips, boat rentals, free docking for your boat with the rental of a cottage, apartment, or room. Restaurants and other facilities are located within walking distance. For more information, contact Silver Sands Motel, RFD 5, Route 11B, Gilford, NH 03246, or call (603) 293-4481.

The Belknap Point Motel, located in Laconia on Route 11, offers rooms on and overlooking Lake Winnipesaukee; contact Milton and Maureen Marsden, Belknap Point Motel, Laconia, NH 03246, or call (603) 293-7511.

Another place to try which offers the convenience of boat rentals, dock, ramp, and cottages right on the lake is the Christmas Island Motel, located five miles north on Route 3. For more information, contact Christmas Island Motel, Laconia, NH 03246, or call (603) 366-4378.

Pick Point Lodges and Cottages are also located on the lake, with a half mile of shorefront and 75 acres of pine forest. Write Box 220A, P.O. Mirror Lake, New Hampshire 03853, or call (603) 569-1338.

There is no closed season on this lake, as with most of New Hampshire's waters, although during the months of May and June, bass may be taken by the use of artificial lures or flies only, and the limit is two fish.

Lake Winnisquam

Winnisquam is 4,264-acre home for both largemouth and smallmouth bass. It is 154 feet deep at its center, and offers some super bass fishing along sharp dropoffs at its shoreline in late summer, using deep-running crankbaits. Early spring fishing is good at the southern (shallower) end of the lake. Try spinners and weighted jellyworms here.

As with Winnipesaukee, boat launching, marinas, and every other kind of service is offered along its shoreline, especially along Route 3.

Winnisquam Beach Campground boasts 150 tent and trailer sites with modern facilities for your stay at the lake. Write The Nickeroons, Box 12N, Lochmere, NH 03252, or call (603) 524-0021.

Paugus Bay

Paugus Bay is connected to Lake Winnisquam on the south by a small neck of water, and to Lake Winnipesaukee on the north by a small inlet of water crossed by Route 11B. Both largemouth and smallmouth bass fishing is excellent all year in the deep and well-oxygenated waters of Paugus Bay. Routes 11 and 3 follow the eastern shoreline; any and all services are available in the area.

Although Paugus has heavy recreational traffic in mid-summer, fishing in the early morning and late afternoon in the area of Moulton's Cove and Quimby Point will cause some excitement when you pick up a lunker that has come in to feed. Paugus Bay should be included in any bass fisherman's trip to the Lakes Region of New Hampshire.

Contoocook River and Lake

Contoocook Lake, just outside Jaffrey off Route 202, is a super bass lake. Largemouth, as well as smallmouth, are in abundance on its 215 acres. The water in the lake is shallow (a maximum of 25 feet) and, as a result, relatively warm. Spring and summer are the best times of the year to fish Contoocook, and the lake produces consistent and excellent results.

A large marsh (over 100 acres) is formed behind the dam at the Contoocook River. This is an excellent area to begin your pursuit of the largemouth. Fish weedless rigged rubber worms in this area, and crankbaits in the deeper half of the lake. Access to Lake Contoocook is gained by a public boat launch off Route 202 in Rindge, NH.

The Contoocook River, which runs out of the lake, extends all the way to Henniker, New Hampshire, running parallel to Route 202 North, and offers over 50 miles of super bass fishing. Except for a small section of the river (from a point marked by signs approximately 2,500 feet above a dam in West Henniker to a point upstream about one mile, also marked by signs) which is closed to all fishing from October 16 to December 31 and limited to the use of single-hooked artificial lures and flies, the river follows the normal state bass regulations.

For the most part, the river is fairly shallow — about 15 feet maximum depth. Small spinner baits are our favorite lures, although we have also had success with live bait and jellyworms.

While canoeing the river, try fishing a four-inch jellyworm, jumping it across the weeds and letting it drop into the little pools along the river bank. The area of the river below the dam is a super spot for picking up your limit in no time.

Monadnock State Park, as mentioned earlier, offers camping facilities in the area of Contoocook Lake.

Emerald Acres Campground, off Route 202, is located on Cheshire Pond near Lake Contoocook. Their 50 tent and trailer sites offer all conveniences. Write D.B. Christian, 71 Ridgecrest Rd., Jaffrey, NH 03452, or call (603) 532-8838.

The Woodbound Inn, located about three miles south on Route 202, then two miles east from there, offers 13 lakefront cottages with fireplaces, boats, canoes, and a boat ramp. For more information, contact Woodbound Inn, Box 311, Jaffrey, NH 03452, or call (603) 532-8341.

New Hampshire's Large Smallmouth Lakes

Some of the more noted New Hampshire lakes are Wentworth, Lake Sunapee, Squam, and Newfound lakes. As mentioned earlier, recent smallmouth bass investigations by the New Hampshire Fish and Game Department have noted a decrease in certain year classes of smallmouth on New Hampshire's larger lakes. Due to these investigations, a change was made in the restrictions on bass fishing in New Hampshire, limiting bass fishing to the use of artificial lures only and the bag limit to two fish during the months of May and June in order to protect spawning bass.

A significant improvement seems already apparent to us, as far as the luck we have had recently on some of these lakes. Strong year classes are now maturing, and we think smallmouth bass fishing on these waters is in for a big comeback over the next few years.

Lake Wentworth

Wentworth Lake, located in Wolfeboro, has an area of over 3,000 acres; it is four miles long and two-and-a-half miles wide. The shoreline is composed of mostly rock, gravel, and sand. There is very little vegetation on this lake except in a few areas of shallows.

Smallmouth bass were first introduced into Wentworth in 1878, and periodic stocking was done until the early 1950s. It seems that an abundance of white perch in this lake offers the bass much competition for food since their dietary likes and dislikes are about the same.

Stamp Act Island in the middle of Wentworth offers a rocky shoreline lined with honey-holes, as do the four other smaller islands.

Crayfish is the best live bait to use here; June and July the best months to fish. Boat launching is available for a small fee at Wentworth State Park on Route 109.

Wolfeboro Campground, located on Route 28N, offers 40 wooded sites with all conveniences. Write The Hamiltons, Haines Hill Road, Wolfeboro 03894, or call (603) 569-4029 or 569-9881.

Lake Sunapee

Lake Sunapee, off Routes 103 and 11 near New London, has been one of the targets of the smallmouth bass investigation, with much the same results as the ones mentioned previously. In creel studies run on the lake in 1981, the bass averaged 11.5 inches in length and 12.7 ounces in weight. This is another New Hampshire smallmouth bass fishery undergoing a comeback.

Sunapee is 4,085 acres of cold water, an exceptional fishery for lake trout and salmon, but smallmouth bass, though sometimes overlooked, is a fishery on the upswing.

The shoreline of Sunapee is developed by summer homes and tourist businesses, and the traffic on the lake can be heavy in the summer; therefore, spring and fall (and dawn and dusk during summer) are your best times to fish.

There are 10 boat launching sites on the lake; one of the best of these is the one at Sunapee State Park at the southern tip of the lake. Although the park does not have a campground, it offers excellent recreational facilities.

Otter Pond Campground in New London is a small campground (28 sites) near Lake Sunapee. It offers all the necessary conveniences. Write Ed and Marge Leskiewicz, Thrasher Road, Claremont 03743 and (in summer) telephone (603) 763-5600.

Rand Pond Campground, located only four miles from Lake Sunapee, is a larger campground (100 sites) offering modern facilities on a 49-acre lake. Contact The Horns, Box 690, Goshen 03752, or call (603) 863-3350.

Indian Cove Lodge, located on Sunapee Harbor, boasts 50 units on the hillside overlooking Lake Sunapee; rooms, and one- or two-bedroom cottages on picturesque grounds. You may rent boats and canoes, and the lodge has docking facilities. Write Box 713, Lake Sunapee 03782, or telephone (603) 763-2762.

Squam Lake

Squam Lake, located at Holderness along Route 3, has an area of over 6,700 acres and is New Hampshire's second largest lake. The maximum depth is 98 feet; the average depth is 36 feet. Squam Lake is bordered on the north by the Squam Mountains, and drains into Little Squam Lake to the southwest. Squam is deep, cold, and clear, with little vegetation. The shoreline is rocky and wooded and the bottom is gravelly and rocky.

Smallmouth bass from Lake Champlain were first introduced into Squam in the 1870s and regular stocking has taken place since. The best places to fish on Squam are the shoreline and island shoals in the central region of the lake and the easterly sections.

Worms, crayfish, hellgrammites, and shiners are the live baits that produce results; use any of their imitations when using artificial lures. Summer traffic is heavy, but early morning and late afternoon fishing produces good results.

If camping is your pleasure, then Ames Brook KOA Campground, situated close to Lake Squam, is a good place to stay. Contact The Parringtons, RR1, Ashland 03217, or call (603) 968-7735.

Situated on Lake Squam, The Olde Colonial Eagle offers 16 units overlooking the lake with rental boats, canoes, and docking available. Write Olde Colonial Eagle, Drawer R, Holderness 03245, or call (603) 968-3233.

Newfound Lake

Newfound Lake, just out of Bristol on Route 3A, is the fourth largest lake in New Hampshire, with over 4,000 acres of water area; it is also one of the deepest, around 180 feet. Much of the lake is over 100 feet deep. Newfound Lake is crystal clear, with a rocky and sandy bottom. Vegetation is very scarce, found mainly at the northern tip of the lake at the mouth of the Cockermouth River. Bass congregate in this area, and in Sandborn Bay to the east.

Once again, crayfish is the best bait on Newfound; June is the best producing month, although July offers good results. The best places to fish are the shoal areas at the mouth of the Fowler River south to Mayhew Island and to the mouth of Black Brook. Fishing around the area of the four islands on Newfound Lake produces good results. There are three commercial boat launches for access to the lake.

Other Information

For those interested in exploring some of the more remote areas of New Hampshire, there are several guide services available; among those, The Pemigewasset Guide Service offers fishing guides for the central and northern New Hampshire areas. They can be contacted at Pemigewasset Guide Service, P.O. Box 502, Plymouth 03264, or call (603) 968-7867.

For more information on licensing and regulations, contact the New Hampshire Fish and Game Department, 34 Bridge Street, Concord 03301.

A Word About Coastal Waters

Fishing the mouths of rivers where they dump into the ocean can be a challenge worth accepting. In the headwaters and drainage basins of the many rivers of New England, the water is somewhat saline and the large-mouth that enter these areas have a whole new variety of food to add to their diet.

The bass in these backwaters will be much harder to catch unless you use a type of bait that resembles the predominant food supply found in these waters. They may be feeding on shrimp, for instance. Clam worms or some other typically salt water food may be the prevalent food supply well back into these backwater areas. Your best bet in these circumstances is to try the lures that resemble these saltwater baits.

The backwaters of Great Bay, Little Bay, and areas of the Piscataqua River offer no end of possibilities for the imaginative fisherman. We have had good luck in this area fishing with jellyworm techniques, using a rubber eel rigged in a weedless fashion.

Fishing the areas of the upper and lower narrows of the Lamprey River, as well as where the Exeter, Oyster, Bellamy, and Winnicut rivers connect with Great Bay, will net you some nice specimens. (Note: There are a number of special regulations enforced in this area regarding shad, salmon, and the like. Check current New Hampshire fishing regulations concerning Great Bay.)

There are no end to services available along Routes 4, 101, and 108. Boat launching sites are available all along Great Bay, particularly along Route 4 in the area of Hilton State Park.

As we found in the chapter on the state of Maine, New Hampshire also has a number of lakes, ponds, and rivers in which bass are found. In the following section, we have endeavored to provide you with a listing of some of the more interesting bass waters to be found in New Hampshire. Some pertinent information, such as the nearest town and route numbers, is contained in each listing, followed by SMB when smallmouth predominates, LMB when largemouth is the species to pursue, or the word "Both" when both species are represented in the particular body of water. The waters preceded by an asterisk are considered to be our "best bets" for those seeking the challenge of an encounter with the black bass.

BELKNAP COUNTY

Bear Pond (Alton): Route 11; LMB; motorboats restricted.

Crystal Lake (Gilmanton): Route 140; 441 acres; 51 feet maximum; May through June; rocky bottom, surface vegetation; free state boat launch at southern tip; SMB.

Gilman Pond (Alton): Route 11; LMB; reclaimed — exclusively LMB here; motorboats restricted.

Halfmoon Lake (Alton, Barnstead): Route 28; 280 acres; 29 feet maximum; May through June; LMB and SMB; small boat and canoe access at outlet on southern tip.

Knights Pond (Alton): Route 11; LMB; reclaimed; motorboats restricted.

Lily Pond (Barnstead, Pittsfield): Route 28, Route 126; LMB; sometimes called Horn Pond.

Lily Pond (Gilford): Exit Route 3 toward Gilford; LMB.

*Manning Lake (Gilmanton Ironworks): North of Route 140 and Crystal Lake; May through season; rocky shore; great LMB and SMB fishing; small boat or canoe launch on northwestern shore.

*Merrymeeting River (Alton, New Durham): Route 11; LMB; restrictions on portions of the river at Alton.

*Pemigewasset Pond (Meredith, New Hampton): Route 104; 241 acres; 30 feet maximum; May through October; noted for excellent bass fishing; campground and boat launching off Route 104.

Silver Lake (Belmont, Northfield, Tilton): Route 3; SMB.

Sunset Lake (Alton, Gilmanton): off Route 11; 206 acres; 62 feet maximum; sometimes called Places Pond; rocky bottom, wooded shoreline — good SMB action near islands and near submerged island near Frohock Brook; boat launching for small boats and canoes.

*Waukewan Lake (Meredith): Route 3, Route 104 crosses southern shoreline; SMB in abundance and crayfish or crayfish artificials is the bait of choice; rocky, gravelly bottom; try shoreline and Chapman Island; boat launch off Route 104.

CARROLL COUNTY

Balch Pond (Wakefield, NH; Newfield, Me.): Route 153; 704 acres; 44 feet maximum; May through June and winter; mainly pickerel but fair LMB and SMB fishing.

Chocorua Lake (Tamworth): Route 16; 222 acres; 28 feet maximum; mid-April through June; motorboats restricted; because of the lake's location close to the mountains, weather is an important factor — watch out for fast-moving storms and wind; excellent SMB fishing; small boat and canoe launch off Route 16.

*Conway Lake (Conway): Route 16, Route 302; May through June; excellent SMB fishing; fish the rocks off Willey Brook area; free state boat ramp at northern tip; canoe launch at southern tip.

Crescent Lake (Wolfeboro): Route 28; SMB.

Dan Hole Pond (Ossipee, Tuftonboro): off Routes 16, 25 — not easy to find; 408 acres; 126 feet maximum; SMB; good fishing in early spring; access through campground; dangerous weather shifts — beware.

*Great East Lake (Wakefield, NH; Acton, Me.): Route 153; 1,686 acres; 102 feet maximum; May through June, September, winter; reclaimed; interstate regulations; SMB and LMB — use deep-running crankbaits; good ice fishing; boat launch off Route 153.

Kanasatka Lake (Moultonboro): Route 25; SMB.

Kingswood Lake (Brookfield): Route 109; SMB.

Kusumpe Pond (Sandwich): Route 113; SMB.

Lovell Lake (Wakefield): Route 109 out of Sanbornville; 538 acres; 41 feet maximum; SMB fishing very good around islands; late April through summer, winter; boat launch at dam.

*Mirror Lake (Tuftonboro, Wolfeboro): Route 109; 377 acres; 44 feet maximum; LMB fishing excellent all season; two boat launches, one on Route 109.

*Ossipee Lake (Ossipee): Route 25 and Route 16; 3,092 acres; 61 feet maximum; late April through season; SMB fishing good in Broad and Leavitt bays; sandy bottom; launch sites off both major routes and camping on the eastern shore of the main lake.

Province Lake (Effingham): Route 153; 1,008 acres; 17 feet maximum; May through summer; LMB and SMB; interstate regulations; shallow and sandy with boat launching facilities off Route 153.

Round Pond (Wakefield): Route 153; SMB; reclaimed.

Rust Pond (Wolfeboro): Route 28; 210 acres; 39 feet maximum; late April through season; SMB; small boat or canoe launch near Route 28 in South Wolfeboro.

*Silver Lake (Madison): Route 41 parallels western shoreline, Route 113 crosses at northern tip; 996 acres; 164 feet maximum; late April through season; excellent SMB fishing — try Big Island to the north and a large cove mid-way down the eastern shore; boat launch at dam on Route 41.

Upper Kimball Pond (Chatham): off Route 113; in scenic White Mountain National Forest; weedy pond; fish deeper mid-section for SMB; small boat launch off northern tip.

CHESHIRE COUNTY

Chesham Pond (Harrisville): north of Route 101; both.

Forest Pond (Winchester): Route 10; LMB.

Frost Pond (Dublin, Jaffrey): Route 137; SMB.

Gilmore Pond (Jaffrey): Route 124; SMB.

Granite Lake (Nelson, Stoddard): Route 9; 211 acres; 101 feet maximum; April through July; rocky and gravelly bottom; good SMB around island; boat launch off Route 9 on southern shore.

*Highland Lake (Stoddard): Route 123 crosses southern tip; 711 acres; 30 feet maximum; LMB fishing is excellent along shallows and weeds in spring — use jellyworms at Upton, Rice, Kennedy, Brooks and Pickerel creeks; fish edges of the many springs in summer; boat launch off Route 123.

Hubbard Pond (Rindge): off Route 119, near Cathedral of the Pines; SMB.

Meetinghouse Pond (Marlboro): Route 101; LMB.

Pearley Lake (Rindge): Route 119; LMB.

Scott Pond (Fitzwilliam): Route 119; LMB.

*Silver Lake (Harrisville, Nelson): Between Routes 9 and 101 east of Keene; 233 acres; 81 feet maximum; mid-April through September; deep, cold lake with exceptional SMB fishing; boat launch on southeastern tip.

*Spofford Lake (Chesterfield): Route 9A parallels eastern shoreline and Route 63 parallels western shore; 707 acres; 60 feet maximum; late April through season; both LMB and SMB fishing good; large northern pike are predators on the bass here; fish dropoffs at Pierce Island and Rocky Point; boat launches off 9A.

*Thorndike Pond (Dublin, Jaffrey): off Route 124, near Monadnock State Park; 265 acres; 18 feet maximum; May through season, winter; shallow, warm water and SMB everywhere — this is a quiet little place to practice the art of bassing; access is a little rough unless you are using a small cartop boat or a canoe.

*Warren Lake (Alstead): Route 123; both.

COOS COUNTY

Forest Lake (Dalton, Whitefield): off Route 116, at Forest Lake State Park; SMB and LMB.

Martin Meadow Pond (Lancaster): Route 3; LMB.

Nay Pond (Milan): Route 110; SMB; reclaimed.

GRAFTON COUNTY

Armington Lake (Piermont): Route 25C; SMB.

Baker Pond (Orford): Route 25A, near Gilman's Corner; SMB; both upper and lower ponds.

*Canaan Street Lake (Canaan): off Route 4-Canaan Center; 303 acres; 20 feet maximum; late April through season; fishing restricted in southeastern arm of lake; excellent LMB and SMB fishing all over the lake; free gravel boat launch on western shore; Crescent Campsites on lake, 60 sites, free use of dock and boat launch area; write Howard and Anita Beloin, P.O. Box 225, Canaan 03741, or call (603) 523-9910.

Crystal Lake (Enfield): Route 4A; 354 acres; 53 feet maximum; SMB and rock bass; May through June; boat launch.

*Grafton Pond (Grafton): off Route 4; 235 acres; 66 feet maximum; 6 h.p. limit on boats; no camping allowed; great SMB fishing in area of rocks on western shore and around islands; free boat launching for small boats near dam.

Indian Pond (Orford): off Route 25A; SMB — nothing but.

*Mascoma Pond (Enfield): Route 4A; 1,115 acres; 68 feet maximum; late May through summer, September, and winter; LMB around any of the many feeder brooks and SMB around islands in spring and deep dropoffs in summer; boat launching either side of bridge on Route 4A; campground on lake.

*Squam Lake, Little (Holderness): Just off Route 3, Route 25 parallels western shoreline; late May through season; Little Squam is connected to Big Squam by Squam River; rocky shoreline with sandy, gravelly bottom; excellent SMB fishing; fish this lake the same as Squam — see main chapter; boat launchings at inlet and outlet to lake.

Stinson Lake (Rumney, Ellsworth): off Route 25 in national forest; 346 acres; 75 feet maximum; late May through season; SMB; no development; boat ramp at dam — fee charged; ice fishing is good.

*Tarleton Lake (Piermont): Route 25C parallels western shoreline; 315 acres; 60 feet maximum; fantastic SMB fishing; locals troll streamers or wet flies for some outstanding action; SMB tend to populate the eastern shoreline; good boat launch for small to medium-sized boats off Route 25C.

HILLSBOROUGH COUNTY

*Deering Reservoir (Deering): Route 149; 315 acres; 35 feet maximum; late April through June and great ice fishing; gravelly bottom; SMB around islands and eastern shore; two boat launches.

Dudley Pond (Deering): north of Route 149; both; electric motors only.

Gould Pond (Hillsborough): Route 202; SMB.

Gregg Lake (Antrim): west off Route 31 out of Clinton Village; SMB.

Haunted Lake (Francestown): Route 136; LMB.

Horace Lake (Weare): off Route 149 or 77, 114; late April through spring; dam construction has caused fishing to suffer; bog in northern part of lake good place for LMB; SMB along dropoffs; fee for parking — launching is free near dam at northern tip; also known as Weare Reservoir.

Hunts Pond (Hancock): Route 123; SMB.

*Merrimack River (Boscawen, Hooksett): Route 3; both; bass fishing is good to excellent in Concord area, near dam at Hooksett, and rocky areas along its length.

Norway Pond (Hancock): Route 137; SMB.

Otter Lake (Greenfield): Route 31, at Greenfield State Park; SMB and LMB.

Otternick Pond (Hudson): Route 111; LMB.

Pierce Lake (Hillsborough): Route 9; SMB.

Pleasant Pond (Francestown): off Route 47; SMB.

Potanopa Pond (Brookline): Route 13; SMB.

Robinson Pond (Hudson): Route 111; LMB.

Shattuck Pond (Francestown): off Route 47; LMB; reclaimed.

Stevens Pond (Manchester): Route 3; both.

Monomac is fair fishing is spring, but some super-sized bass are caught in early summer and mid-fall.

MERRIMACK COUNTY

Blaisdell Lake (Sutton): Route 114; SMB.

Bradley Lake (Andover): Route 4; SMB.

*Chestnut Pond (Epsom): north of Route 9; LMB.

Clement Pond (Hopkinton): north of Route 9; SMB; also called Joe Silver Lake.

Crooked Pond (Loudon): Route 129; LMB.

Forest Pond (Canterbury): Route 132; both.

Gorham Pond (Dunbarton): Route 13; LMB.

Highland Lake (Andover): Route 11; 211 acres; 48 feet maximum; late April through July; SMB fishing along dropoffs good; sandy to clay bottom; paved boat ramp off Route 11.

Kezar Lake (Sutton): Route 114; both.

*Little Sunapee Lake (New London): Exit 12 off Route 89, Route 11 parallels southern shore; 472 acres; 43 feet maximum; late April through season; SMB fishing particularly good around Colby Point, a jut of land that nearly bisects the lake; small boat launch off Route 11.

*Massasecum Lake (Bradford): Route 114; 402 acres; 50 feet maximum; excellent SMB fishing all season and in winter; shoreline varies between rocky and weedy; SMB congregate around large island to the south and the eastern shoreline; boat launching and camping off Route 114.

Odiorne Pond (Epsom): Route 9; LMB.

*Pleasant Lake (New London): Route 11; 606 acres; 91 feet maximum; May through season; has held the SMB state record in the past; wooded and rocky shoreline; SMB can be picked up all along the shoreline; commercial launch site with services available and there is a free launch site off Route 11.

Pleasant Pond (Henniker): off Route 114; LMB; reclaimed.

Turkey Pond, Big (Concord): Route 13; LMB.

*Turtletown Pond (Concord): Route 132; LMB; some monster bass out of here in years past.

*Webster Lake (Franklin): Route 11 passes southern shoreline; 612 acres; 40 feet maximum; good SMB fishing on northeastern and western shoreline at dropoffs May, June, July; boat launch at two town beaches — fee charged.

*Winnepocket Lake (Webster): off Route 127; 627 acres; 55 feet maximum; May, June through summer; excellent SMB fishing in clear water using small spinnerbaits; crankbaits in mid-summer; boat launch at outlet.

ROCKINGHAM COUNTY

*Bow Lake (Strafford): Route 202A; 1,160 acres; 75 feet maximum; mid-April through June; excellent SMB fishing especially along shoreline on eastern side of lake; three boat launching sites.

Beaver Lake (Derry): Route 102; SMB.

*Canobie Lake (Salem, Windham): Route 111A; 304 acres; 44 feet maximum; home of Canobie Lake Amusement Park; LMB along southern shoreline in shallows; SMB along dropoffs on eastern shoreline; boat launching off Route 111A.

*Exeter River (Chester and Newmarket): along Routes 111 and 102; excellent fishing for both LMB and SMB along entire length but particularly

Lake Monomac is located on the border of New Hampshire and Massachusetts, and offers good bassin' a short drive from major eastern cities.

the lower stretches where the river is wider; rubber weedless rigged eels work wonders here.

Harvey Lake (Northwood): Route 9; LMB.

Island Pond (Atkinson, Derry, Hempstead): Routes 111, 121; 510 acres; 79 feet maximum; late April through summer, September; SMB and LMB around shoreline of large island in middle of lake; best to use fee-charged boat launch near dam.

Jenness Lake (Northwood): Route 107; 243 acres; 28 feet maximum; there are plenty of SMB but their size is small; bottom sandy in some areas and muddy in others; boat launch off Route 107.

North River Pond (Northwood, Barrington, Nottingham): Route 202; SMB.

**Northwood Lake (Northwood): Route 4; 687 acres; 24 feet maximum; May through summer and September; excellent bass fishing for both species; LMB tend to congregate in the western weedier part of the lake and both species are found along western shoreline and dropoffs; three boat launches — all charge fees.

Onway Lake (Raymond): Route 102; LMB and SMB; reclaimed.

Phillips Pond (Sandown): Route 121A; both.

Pleasant Lake (Deerfield): Route 107; SMB.

Scobie Pond (Londonderry): Route 28; SMB.

Shingle Pond (Deerfield): Route 43; LMB.

Taylor Pond (Hampton): Route 1; LMB.

STRAFFORD COUNTY

*Ayers Pond (Barrington): Route 202; 228 acres; 40 feet maximum; all season; both LMB and SMB; excellent bass fishing especially along eastern shoreline; state boat launch site above the dam off Route 202 and a small boat or canoe site at northern tip; campsites along Route 202.

**Lamprey River (Deerfield to Newmarket): Routes 125, 101, 107; 43 miles of excellent river fishing for both LMB and SMB; the section of river above Wiswall Dam and the section below Packers Falls are without a doubt two of the best bass fishing spots in all of New Hampshire.

Lily Pond (Somersworth): off Route 16; SMB.

Mendums Pond (Barrington): Route 4; both.

*Merrymeeting Lake (New Durham): off Route 11; 1,111 acres; 122 feet maximum; SMB in late spring through summer; water is very clear, very little vegetation; SMB may be taken near brooks on southwestern and northeastern shoreline; two boat launching sites near dam.

Suncook Lakes, Upper and Lower (Barnstead): Route 28; 216 acres in lower lake; 15 feet maximum; 362 acres in upper lake; 41 feet maximum; both lakes connected by a narrow strait; perch are taking over here and though the SMB fishing is good now, it may be affected in the future; boat launching along narrow connecting strait.

Sunrise Pond (Middleton): Route 153; LMB.

*Swains Pond (Barrington): off Route 9; 520 acres; 29 feet maximum; excellent LMB fishing but SMB are here, too; rocky shoreline; good boat launches, especially off Mica Point.

Wheelwright Pond (Lee): Route 125; SMB.

SULLIVAN COUNTY

*Ashuelot Pond (Washington): off Route 31; 428 acres; 21 feet maximum; May first through June, winter; both; fly fish only on south branch, Swanzey, Troy and from bridge in East Swanzey to Farrar Pond Dam; fish rocky areas for SMB and muddy, weedy areas (Ashuelot River) for LMB; gravel boat ramp; ice fishing here is very good.

Crescent Lake (Acworth, Unity): north of Route 123A; SMB.

*Island Pond (Washington): off Route 31; noted for exceptional LMB and SMB fishing all season; try area of weeds on southern arm and around islands; boat launch on southern tip.

Kolelemook Lake (Springfield): off Route 4A; both.

May Pond (Washington): Route 31; LMB.

Perkins Pond (Sunapee): off Route 11; SMB.

Bowdish Reservoir in the George Washington Management Area features the shallow backwater bass love.

CHAPTER **12**

RHODE ISLAND

Worden Pond — Indian Lake — Flat River
Reservoir — Stafford Pond — Belleville Pond —
Pausacaco Pond — other favorites by county.

"The biggest little state in the Union," Rhode Island is home to the Americas Cup Races and famous for its delicious cornmeal Johnny Cakes. While most noted for its salt water sports, this little state also has a freshwater management program that promotes bass fishing in its inland waters.

Rhode Island's lakes and ponds are, for the most part, shallow. Many of the ponds are man-made, constructed in the 1800s for use in textile and other industries. The water is soft and very low in alkalinity and some ponds are limited in the number of fish they can support. The highly developed areas surrounding many of Rhode Island's ponds and lakes tend to accelerate weed growth which often becomes a problem for boaters and fishermen. For the most part, though, shallow and weedy waters are largemouth territory and many, if not most, of Rhode Island's waters host old mossyback.

Once noted for fine smallmouth fisheries, Rhode Island has seen the largemouth take over its lakes and ponds due, in part, to the illegal stocking of this species. Smallmouth bass from the Great Lakes were stocked in Rhode Island shortly after the Civil War. Largemouth were introduced some time later and have become widespread. Good smallmouth fisheries still exist in Indian Lake in South Kingston and in Stafford Pond in Tiverton.

The spawning season for largemouth in Rhode Island is usually early June, while the spawning season for smallmouth occurs late in May or early in June. As is sometimes the case in Rhode Island's shallow ponds, temperature variations in the water can cause a split spawning season. The size limit on largemouth bass was removed in the mid-1960s and creel limits were set to extend the harvest over a longer time.

Both the largemouth and the smallmouth tend to feed on insects, crayfish, and small fish of various species in this state; consequently, flies of various sorts, crayfish artificials, and any of the Rebel™ and Rapala™ lures, especially the broken-back shiner imitations, work well here.

147

There is no creel limit in effect on Stafford Pond at this time and the limit is five bass, either smallmouth or largemouth, or in the aggregate on all other fresh waters in Rhode Island. *Always check for new regulations or changes in regulations before embarking on your trip.*

Worden Pond

Located in South Kingston abutting the Great Swamp Management Area, Worden Pond is noted for being one of the best bass fishing areas in the state. To get to Worden Pond, take Route 110 to Tuckerton, then follow the Wordens Pond Road which crosses the southern shoreline.

The 1,075 acres of Worden Pond are shallow (average depth of four feet), but a good circulation of water keeps the pond adequately oxygenated. The edges of the pond are marshy and swampy, providing good breeding grounds. Fishing the edges of these areas with weedless artificials makes for good bass fishing.

Parking, docking, and boat launching facilities are located along the Wordens Pond Road. Places to stay during your visit here abound as you travel the few miles to the Block Island Sound beach areas.

Indian Lake

Traveling east from Worden Pond along Route 138, we come to Route 1 South, which passes to the east of another great bass pond, Indian Lake.

The growth rates of both largemouth and smallmouth in Indian Lake exceed the state averages, and the lake appears to have a good balance between predators and forage fish.

Largemouth were introduced without authorization in the mid 1950s, and Indian Lake has seen a decrease in smallmouth populations ever since. Smallmouth are still here in good numbers, though, and the largemouth are thriving.

Over its 221 acres, Indian Lake has an average depth of seven feet. Many rubber artificials work well here, particularly a rubber eel rigged weedless fashion and tossed in the shallows along the perimeter of the lake.

There is a state boat launching ramp on the south end of the pond, and the Holiday Inn of South Kingston is located at the junction of Routes 1 and 138 just north of the lake. The telephone number for reservations is (401) 789-1051.

Flat River Reservoir

Flat River Reservoir, sometimes called Johnson Pond, runs neck-and-neck with Worden Pond for the title of best bass fishing spot in Rhode Island. This manmade reservoir, located in Coventry just north of the junc-

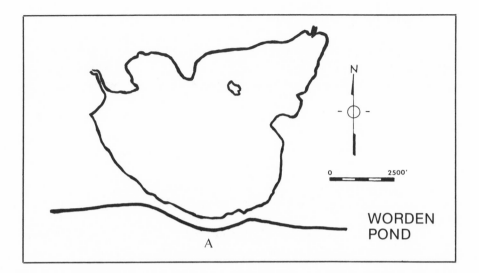

WORDEN
POND

A

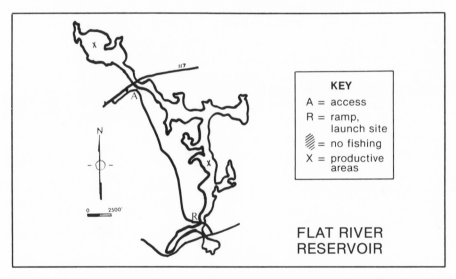

KEY

A = access

R = ramp,
    launch site

= no fishing

X = productive
    areas

FLAT RIVER
RESERVOIR

tion of I-95 and Route 3, covers 659 acres and is relatively deep for a Rhode Island water, with a 36-foot maximum depth and an average depth of 8.5 feet.

Route 117, called Flat River Road, runs north of the reservoir; there is boating access at Zeke's Bridge on Harkney Hill Road where it intersects with Hill Farm Road on the southern arm of the reservoir. There are also private boat launchings in various places around the perimeter.

The area around Flat River Reservoir is highly developed and experiences heavy fishing and recreational use. There is an abundance of forage fish, which accounts for the above average growth rate of game fish.

This is an excellent body of water for night fishing; the jitterbug is the preferred lure here, although any of the noisemakers will work well. During the daytime, fish the dropoffs in the middle area of the reservoir, and the eastern arm.

There are no marinas on the reservoir, but food, lodging, and other services are nearby.

Stafford Pond

The only pond in Rhode Island that has a large population of smallmouth bass, Stafford Pond in Tiverton (in northeastern Newport County) covers 476 acres.

Take Route 195 to Fall River, Massachusetts, then Route 24 to Route 81, which passes the eastern shores of Stafford Pond. Here you will find a state boat launching site and parking areas.

Studies done in the late 1970s showed no largemouth present in Stafford. There are fears that, if largemouth were introduced illegally here, the smallmouth population would be reduced drastically, as has happened in other Rhode Island ponds. But smallmouth fishing can be very interesting in Stafford Pond and large fish have been taken recently.

A natural body of water, unlike many in Rhode Island, it has a maximum depth of 24 feet, averaging 10 feet. The area around the eastern and western shoreline drops off steeply, and can be fished with medium and deep runners during summer. Fly fishing in the early morning and late afternoon in the southern shallows can also be productive.

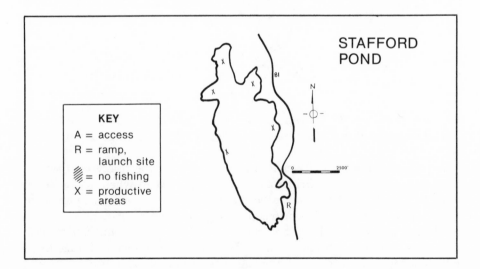

STAFFORD
POND

N

KEY
A = access
R = ramp,
    launch site
= no fishing
X = productive
    areas

Belleville Pond

If you follow Route 1 north from Indian Lake up to North Kingston, you will find Belleville Pond, another of Rhode Island's better bass ponds. This 159-acre pond is fairly shallow, with an average depth of five feet. The shallows are very weedy, but the slightly deeper central area of the pond is not, making it easier to fish.

Belleville Pond is noted for its larger-than-average bass, and Rhode Island's Fish and Game Department is trying to promote the game fisheries in this pond. They have installed a fish ladder at the Annaquatucket River to allow alewives access to Belleville to spawn. With the addition of young alewives as a forage food, it is hoped that the bass fishery will become even better.

A dirt road runs from Oak Hill Road to town land and access to the lake. Fish the edges of the weeds with rubber weedless lures and watch 'em jump!

Pausacaco Pond

Sometimes called Gilbert Stuart Pond, Pausacaco Pond is one of the best warm water fishing areas in the state of Rhode Island. Unless you can obtain a landowner's permission, access is limited to a boat livery at Gilbert Stuart's Birthplace, which can be reached by taking Route 1 to Gilbert Stuart Road.

Sea run alewives spawn in Pausacaco, giving largemouth an excellent diet on which to grow fat and stay healthy.

Even though fishing pressure is light, some monster bass are taken out of here each year. The pond is loaded with large bass and almost anything will entice them to the hook, particularly a weedless rigged eel or medium runners.

The 68-acre pond gradually drops off to a 22-foot maximum depth at the center. This center hole is worth investigating with deep runners and heavier spinnerbaits during mid-summer.

Other Noteworthy Ponds and Lakes

KENT COUNTY

*Carr Pond (West Greenwich): from Route 3 to Division Road to Carr Pond Road; 80 acres; 35 feet maximum; a deep clear pond with rocky shoreline and a sandy bottom make this an excellent pond for SMB, but LMB introduced illegally here have contributed to a reduction of this species' population; even so, fishing for both species here is good and medium to deep runners used in summer will produce pleasing results as will early spring and late fall fishing in the shallows and coves; access is off Carr Pond Road.

Gorton Pond (Warwick): Route 5, Route 1; 62 acres; 45 feet maximum; heavy algae blooms in summer make this a pond to fish in spring; a large panfish population dominates the pond but largemouth fishing is average; plans for a fish ladder in the Apponaug River promises a sea run alewife population to enhance the game fish population; access through city land on south shore of pond.

Mishnock Pond (West Greenwich): Exit 6 off Route 95 to Route 3, then Mishnock Road; both LMB and SMB present here although the SMB are in very low numbers; heavy weeds; cartop boats can be launched off Mishnock Road.

Tiogue Lake (Coventry): Route 3; 215 acres; 11 feet maximum; heavy weeds; the pond is drawn down periodically to control fish populations and weed growth; bass fishing is good and both species are present; access from Route 3 and state boat launch off Arnold Road.

*Warwick Pond (Warwick): off Alternate Route 117, Warwick Avenue, near airport; 83 acres; 26 feet maximum; LMB above state averages, and SMB are present; fishing the inlets and outlets produces results as the alewife population is an abundant game fish food here; access off Warwick Avenue.

BRISTOL COUNTY

*Brickyard Pond (Barrington): Maple Avenue off Route 103; 102 acres; 18 feet maximum; this pond was originally a clay pit and has darker, murkier water than other Rhode Island ponds. Sea run alewives spawn here and provide the better than average LMB fishery with plenty of food. Although use of outboard motors is prohibited here, trolling with an electric and using alewife imitations in season will net you a decent catch. Boat launching is available at the end of West Street from Maple Avenue in Veteran's Memorial Park.

WASHINGTON COUNTY

*Alton Pond and the Wood River (Hopkinton): Route 91; 39 acres; 13 feet maximum; this pond, part of the Wood River system, has heavy weed growth and an overabundance of smaller young fish. LMB fishing is good but they are of a small size; state boat launching on southwestern corner of pond on Route 91; rubber eels and jellyworms rigged in weedless fashion work well here.

*Ashville Pond (Hopkinton): off Route 3 on Canonchet Road; 25 acres; 12 feet maximum; located in the Rockville Management Public Fishing

Area, Ashville Pond was reclaimed in 1960 and 1962 to eliminate chub suckers and restocked with SMB. The reclamations were not totally successful but the addition of northern pike to control the sucker population is hoped to add balance and promote the SMB fishery; boat launching off Canonchet Road.

*Barber Pond (South Kingston): off Route 2; 28 acres; 19 feet maximum; the state LMB record of 9¾ pounds was taken in Barber Pond and both LMB and SMB are taken here and some pretty heavy fish are caught; again rubber weedless worms and spinnerbaits work well; boat launching off Route 2.

Beach Pond (Exeter, RI and Volunton, Ct.): Route 165; 419 acres; 65 feet maximum; this pond was reclaimed in 1959 by Connecticut and Rhode Island to try to establish a good trout pond. Every kind of trout was stocked after reclamation but area residents have illegally stocked the lake with SMB and LMB which have developed an increasing population here; parking and shore fishing on Rhode Island side and boat launching on Connecticut side.

*Breakheart Pond (West Greenwich, Exeter): off Route 95 on Austin Farm Road; 45 acres; 7 feet maximum; located in Arcadia Management Area, Breakheart Pond is very shallow but with good water flow from two brooks. LMB is the dominant species here and large ones are caught often; again, rubber weedless lures are good here off the weeds and spinners in moving water; boat launching access is located off Austin Farm Road.

Browning Mill Pond, sometimes called Arcadia Pond (Exeter, Richmond): off Nooseneck Hill Road from Route 165; 46 acres; 6 feet maximum; this pond should be fished in early spring before the heavy weed growth takes over the entire basin; heavy populations of panfish here but LMB populations are average; access located in Arcadia Park.

Canob Pond (Richmond): Route 138; 10 acres; 9 feet maximum; LMB present in good numbers; very weedy — fish early in the season with weedless rigs; access from Route 138.

*Chapman Pond (Westerly): Route 91, called Westerly Bradford Road; 164 acres; 4 feet maximum; undeveloped shoreline and extremely shallow; large panfish population but good LMB fishing here; boat launching off Westerly Bradford Road.

Deep Pond (Charlestown): Route 1 to Kings Factory Road; 19 acres; 33 feet maximum; this pond is being heavily managed as a trout pond because of its favorable oxygen content; a varying population of LMB exists here; boat launching off Kings Factory Road.

*Locustville Pond (Hopkinton): Fairview Road off Route 3 out of Hope Valley; 83 acres; 12 feet maximum; heavily weeded and heavily fished for LMB during summer months; early a.m. and late p.m. best times to fish; boat launch off Fairview Road.

Schoolhouse Pond (Charlestown): off Kings Factory Road off Route 1; 83 acres; 28 feet maximum; the northern half of the pond drops off gradually to a deep hole; the southern half is shallower with several deeper spots worth investigating during mid-summer; state boat launching off Kings Factory Road.

Silver Spring Lake (North Kingstown): off Route 1; heavily fished for trout in spring; best for bass in summer and fall; state boat launching off Route 1.

Tucker Pond (South Kingstown): off Route 110 on Tuckertown Road; LMB prevalent in summer at 10-14 feet water depth; state boat launching off Tuckertown Road.

*Watchaug Pond (Charlestown): off Route 1 in Burlingame State Park; 573 acres; 36 feet maximum; there are 755 campsites in the park; LMB growth rates here were above state averages and a remnant population of SMB has been reported; boat launching and other facilities at State Park.

PROVIDENCE COUNTY

*Bowdish Reservoir (Glocester): off Route 44; 226 acres; 11 feet maximum; located in George Washington Management Area, Bowdish is very weedy and has a number of floating islands. There is an overpopulation of bluegills and sunfish but the LMB here are of average size and can be taken with weedless rubber worms; the Management Area has 72 campsites, access to the lake, and a boat launching facility; Sunset Cove Bait and Boat Rentals is located on Route 44.

Clarkeville Pond (Glocester): off Route 44 on Coldspring Trail; 13 acres; 12.5 feet maximum; heavily weeded and dominated by pan fish with an average LMB population; boat launching off Route 44 on Coldspring Trail.

*Georgiaville Pond (Smithfield): off Route 104; 92 acres; 25 feet maximum; the growth rates for LMB population here were above average; fish northern shallows in spring and around islands where the bottom drops off in summer; cartop boat launching available at Town Beach.

Herring Pond also called Spring Lake (Burrillville): off Route 102 on Spring Lake Road in Black Hut Management Area; 96 acres; 21 feet maximum; rocky bottom, gravel and hard mud and clear water; once a beautiful SMB pond, Spring Lake has given over to LMB; there is a state boat launching on the lake but no outboards are allowed.

*John L. Curran Upper Reservoir (Cranston): off Route 12 on Seven Mile Road; 30 acres; 17 feet maximum; sandy to muddy bottom, a nearly neutral pH and good oxygen to the 10-foot level, this pond was reclaimed in 1964 and stocked with LMB; in 1969 the LMB population was estimated to be from 9,000 to 14,000 fish; such large numbers mean smaller average size but with an increase in competitive species such as yellow perch the bass population should level out and become more normal; this is a great pond for hot and heavy action all season; state boat launching on Seven Mile Road.

Keech Pond (W. Glocester): take Chestnut Hill Road off Route 44; 129 acres; 14 feet maximum; shallow, very weedy and highly developed shoreline; LMB succumb to weedless rigged worms; state boat launch off Chestnut Hill Road; 10 H.P. limit on outboards.

Mashapaug Pond (Cranston): off Niantic Avenue; 69 acres; 17 feet maximum; muddy bottom and turbid water; has a good LMB population; state boat launching off Niantic Avenue.

Oak Swamp Reservoir (Johnston): Route 6 and Reservoir Avenue; 105 acres; 10 feet maximum; bottom sandy, gravelly and some mud; vegetation limited to shoal areas; pick LMB out of these areas with spinnerbaits; access from Route 6 and Reservoir Avenue and a boat livery on the reservoir.

Olney Pond (Lincoln): off Route 146 in Lincoln Woods State Park; 120 acres; 15 feet maximum; LMB and SMB both present; Olney is presently stocked for trout; state boat launching facility and parking in State Park.

*Pascoag Reservoir, also called Echo Lake (Burrillville, Glocester): off Route 44; 351 acres; 19 feet maximum; heavily developed; best to fish early a.m. and late p.m.; state boat launching off Jackson Schoolhouse Road; live bait shop sells fishing licenses a mile or so down Reservoir Road; Echo Lake Campground on Knibb Road off Eagle Peck Road — signs from Route 100.

Ponagansett Reservoir (Glocester): take Snake Hill Road from Route 102; 223 acres; 31 feet maximum; deep, clear, gravelly bottom; fish shallows in western arm of reservoir for LMB; better plan on a cartop boat, facilities for launching off Snake Hill Road are poor.

Lake Champlain — one of New England's top bass waters.

CHAPTER 13

VERMONT

Lake Champlain — Lake Bomoseen — Lake
Iroquois — Lake Carmi — Lake Fairlee — Lake St.
Catherine — The Connecticut River —
other favorites by county.

The Green Mountain State offers some of the most luscious scenery in
New England. The rolling deep green hills and the hidden little fertile val-
leys give Vermont a storybook quality unequaled anywhere. The people
of Vermont are the most friendly and hospitable we have met in our travels.

The four seasons are reflected at their best in this state — the deep green
foliage of summer, the breathtaking colors of fall, the thick white snowy
carpet of winter, the clean, crisp rebirth at springtime. The fresh, unspoiled
grandeur of the countryside is due in part to the forward-thinking environmental laws established in Vermont to protect its scenic beauty.

Vermont's fish and game laws are also designed to protect these valuable
sporting resources. The regulations have paid off in unspoiled lakes, ponds,
and rivers that are a fisherman's paradise — some just minutes from New
England's major cities.

It has been a hard task to select the best bass waters in Vermont from
over 500 lakes and ponds and some 5,000 miles of fishable streams. Certainly, we will not have covered them all in these pages, and those we do
mention should only be a guide as to where to begin your exploration of
Vermont's bass hotspots.

Lake Champlain

If you visit Vermont for no other reason than to fish Lake Champlain,
you will have made a trip well worth the effort. Lake Champlain is the
sixth largest freshwater lake in the continental United States; for this reason,
it is often called the sixth Great Lake. Lake Champlain starts in Whitehall,
New York and flows north for 110 miles to become the Richelieu River in
southern Quebec, Canada. The border between New York State and Vermont is the deep-water channel in the middle of this lake.

Of the 435 square miles of area that is Lake Champlain, 270 are in the state of Vermont, 150 are in New York, and only 15 are in Quebec. The maximum width of the lake is 12 miles as it spreads out in the rich Champlain Valley between the Green Mountains on the east and the Adirondacks on the west. The maximum depth is 400 feet, in the vicinity of South Ferrisburg, Vermont. In all, the lake includes some 8,234 square miles of drainage area, with 585 miles of shoreline.

There are bridges located at Chimney Point, South Hero, and West Swanton, Vermont and ferries operate between Grand Isle, Vermont and Plattsburgh, New York; Burlington, Vermont and Port Kent, New York; and Charlotte, Vermont and Essex, New York.

The lake is patrolled by the Vermont State Police, the New York County Sheriff and the United States Coast Guard. The Coast Guard monitors radio frequency 156.8 MHz 2 FM and CB channel 9 if you should need assistance while boating on Lake Champlain.

The weather is forecast continually on 162 MHz, and it is a good idea to keep up with the situation weatherwise. Strong winds blowing from north to south can turn beautiful crystal clear Lake Champlain into an angry sea. It is best, at these times, to let the wind subside and moor your boat at one of the many marinas along its shores or, at the very least, anchor your boat, with the appropriate anchor lights, in the lee of any cove out of the area of navigable waters.

There are six special anchorage areas: Ticonderoga, New York; Essex, New York; Shelburne, Vermont; St. Albans, Vermont and two at Mallets Bay, Vermont.

It is also a must to obtain charts #14781, 14782, 14783, 14784, and 14785 of Lake Champlain; they can be obtained at marinas around the lake and in book stores throughout Vermont. These maps contain valuable information for those boating on the lake.

There are three particularly dangerous areas on the lake — the Burlington Breakwall, Rock Dunder, and the Colchester Reef. Your charts will help you locate them.

You must have suitable flotation devices on board — one for each person — and be sure to check at the marina for the latest coast guard regulations and information before embarking on your fishing trip. Remember, Lake Champlain is like a small sea; if you treat this monster lake with respect, however, she will reward you with many pleasant and memorable hours of bass fishing.

The largemouth bass in Champlain average two to three pounds, with four- and five-pounders being caught quite often. A six-plus-pounder is trophy size, and there are many of these fellows out there — you just have to find them!

The lake has a large stable bass population just waiting for a tangle with a talented fisherman. The season opens the second Saturday in June and runs through late fall. *Be sure to check your regulations handbook for the exact dates.* The first few weeks of the season after the bass have spawned, when they are found in the shallows, are often the best. From late July through early September, the larger bass will be found in deep water and will come in to feed in the shallows only after dark. In the fall, they will come in to the shallows to feed until the chill of late fall forces them into the warmer holes in deep water.

The best fishing times all season are early morning and late evening. Early in the season, the bass will be found at the edges of marshes and weed beds in the coves and bays. Some of the best areas to try are the mouths of the Lamoille and the Missisquoi rivers and Otter Creek.

In the summer, fish after dark in the shallows and in the early morning and evening over slightly deeper weedy areas and at the edges of weedbeds.

Our best experiences have been with chartreuse or all-black spinnerbaits and a six-inch blue Mister Twister™ rubber worm, fished in the shallows. Purple is another good color for rubber worms. Surface noisemakers work well after dark, and deep-running crankbaits and jig and eel combinations are winners in deep water.

When it comes to live bait, four- to six-inch shiners still-fished in the shallows are our favorites, although crayfish, crawlers, and frogs are great also.

Smallmouth bass are abundant in Lake Champlain, especially in the northern half. They usually weigh from two to three pounds; four-pounders are seen quite often, with five-plus-pounders out there for the lucky fisherman.

The season for smallmouth is the same as for largemouth, and fishing is good all day and all through the season. As with largemouth, smallmouth fishing is best during the early morning and late evening and after dark, with smallmouth sticking to deep water during the day and coming back into the shallows after dark.

Unlike the largemouth, the smallmouth prefer submerged rocky shoals and points along the shore and islands rather than the weedier sections of the lake. In springtime, you will find them in five to 10 feet of water; in the summer, fish around rocky reefs and points. At night, fish the rocky shallows. In the fall, you will find them all over the lake, but in cold weather they will head back into deep water.

The best baits by far to use on the Lake Champlain smallmouth are crayfish and crayfish artificials. Fish these (as well as small Rapalas™ and small surface plugs) along the shoreline in the early morning and late evening and after dark throughout the summer.

Trolling is a good tactic for covering a large water like Lake Champlain.

In mid-summer and late fall, live bait, such as crayfish, shiners, and nightcrawlers, fished near the bottom in a school of bronzebacks, will produce some fast action.

One excellent way to fish for smallmouth in the spring on Lake Champlain is to fly fish in the shallows, using a large bushy dry fly or surface bass bugs. Because smallmouth feed on insect hatches in the early morning, late evening, and after dark, fly fishing can be a real treat on Lake Champlain.

Ice fishing on Champlain is excellent, also. In wintertime, little villages of huts spring up in various areas of the lake. Check your Vermont regulations for seasons and other restrictions. Be careful, too. Because of Champlain's size, there are many winters when the ice does not set in completely over the lake. It is best to check with the local tackle shops for the latest information on conditions before setting out on your ice fishing trip.

Remember when you fish this lake that a New York license is required to fish the western side of the lake, while a Vermont license is required for fishing the eastern side.

Lake Champlain offers no end of areas to fish for bass but three of the better spots that we have enjoyed are:

1. North of where Route 2 crosses from the Vermont mainland to the string of islands, including Grande Isle in the northern half of the lake. Both largemouth and smallmouth abound here, and they stay in the shallows most summers. There are lots of water plants in this area; buzzing a light spinnerbait around and through the weeds produces great results. The western side of the islands is also good.

2. The Canadian border splits Missisquoi Bay in half; this is an area of Lake Champlain filled with largemouth. From Chapman's Bay to Ransoms Bay on the western side of the Missisquoi National Wildlife Refuge, and in Goose Bay on the eastern side of the Refuge, smallmouth abound. There is a boat ramp at West Swanton, Vermont on Route 78 and another at Rock River on Route 7.

3. Mallets Bay and the mouth of the Lamoille River in the area of Colchester, Vermont is an excellent area for both largemouth and smallmouth. From Sand Bar State Park to Mallets Bay and south to Colchester Point, the shoreline holds some trophy-sized bass. Fish for largemouth at the mouth of the Lamoille, at the entrance to Mallets Bay and around the islands in that area, and in the coves along the northern shoreline of the bay. Hunt the smallmouth on the western shore of the lake across from the mouth of the Lamoille, in and around Coates Island in Mallets Bay, and on the eastern shore of the bay.

It would take a whole book in itself to list the lodgings, marinas, and other services available in the Lake Champlain area. But we have listed some of the major state parks and private campgrounds situated near the better bass fishing spots on the lake to help you more easily locate a good spot to stay on your trip. We have also listed in the appendix of this book some addresses to write to for more information on the Lake Champlain area.

If you visit Vermont for fishing and neglect Lake Champlain, you have not visited Vermont. This has got to be the best freshwater fishing area in the Northeast for every kind of fisherman, including bass fishermen.

Private Campgrounds

Campbell's Bay Campground
Alec and Susan Campbell
RFD 2
Swanton, VT 05488
Tel. (802) 868-7258 or 868-4673

Champlain Valley Campground
Marcel and Jienette Gagne
Box 391
RD 1
Swanton, VT 05488
Tel. (802) 524-5146

Dutch Bay Campground
Al and Shirley Engelhardt
North Hero, VT
Tel. (802) 372-8233

Lone Pine Campsites, Inc.
Henry and Rose Miles, Managers
Mallets Bay
Colchester, VT 05446
Tel. (802) 878-5447

Mallets Bay Campground
Lawrence and Phyllis Gregoire
Colchester, VT 05446
Tel. (802) 863-6980

Silent Cedars Campground
Larry and Esther Steeneck, Managers
Grande Isle, VT 05458
Tel. (802) 372-5938

State Parks with Camping Facilities

Button Bay State Park
RFD #3
Vergennes, VT 05491
Tel. (802) 475-2377

D.A.R. State Park
RFD #3
Vergennes, VT 05491
Tel. (802) 759-2354 or 773-2733

Grande Isle State Park
Grande Isle, VT 05458
Tel. (802) 372-4300 or 372-5060

North Hero State Park
North Hero, VT 05474
Tel. (802) 372-8727 or 372-5060

State Parks with Boat Launching Facilities

Kill Kare State Park
St. Albans Bay, VT 05481
Tel. (802) 524-6021 or 372-5060

Knight Point State Park
North Hero, VT 05474
Tel. (802) 372-8389 or 372-5060

Lake Bomoseen

All 2,739 acres of Lake Bomoseen offer recreational opportunities galore; the fishing here is excellent! Facilities abound in the area, with cottages for rent around the lake, and lodging, including a Country Bed and Breakfast, on Float Bridge Road off Route 30, which parallels the lake on the eastern shore. Inns, restaurants, general stores, tackle shops, and any other service you may require — all are found on the shores of this lake, on Route 30 or on Creek Road, which parallels the western shore.

Fishing access is available on Creek Road on the southwestern shore and on Johnson-Spooner Road to the east of Loves Marsh Waterfowl Refuge Area, as well as at Bomoseen State Park and various other points along the lake.

Lake Bomoseen was once the very "in" place to go for wealthy and famous vacationers, and is still a top resort area in Vermont.

Bomoseen State Park has 65 campsites set in a wildlife refuge, and offers an excellent naturalist program and boat rentals.

Lake Bomoseen Campground, situated on Route 30, four and a half miles north of Route 4, is open from May 1 to late September, and offers 85 wooded sites on 33 acres right on the lake. Bait and tackle, as well as boat and motor rentals, are available here. Contact Rod and Pat Holzworth, Route 30, Lake Bomoseen, 05732, or call (802) 273-2061.

Fishing is excellent for both bass species, particularly in the southern part of the lake and in the bays and coves all around the perimeter. The shallower, weedier northern arm of the lake is bass heaven during the spring and fall, and will be sure to satisfy your bass fever urges.

For a wealth of information about the lake, contact the Lake Bomoseen Association, Castleton 05735.

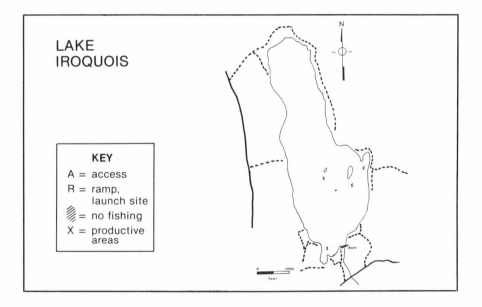

Lake Iroquois

Nestled in a valley in Chittenden County, not far from Lake Champlain, in the towns of Williston and Hinesburg, Lake Iroquois' 254 acres sprawl 1.4 miles in length. About 100 summer and year-round homes dot the lake, mostly on the southern end.

The lake's maximum depth is 37 feet, with an average depth of 20 feet. A small inlet to the lake is located on the northern end of the lake, but like many Vermont lakes, Lake Iroquois is mainly spring-fed, with the water level maintained by a 90-foot-long dam at the southern tip, owned by the Iroquois Manufacturing Company. The Vermont Fish and Game Department maintains a boating access off Pond Road on Lumpity Lane on the northwestern shore. Algae blooms and weeds cover the northern shallower end of the lake in deep summer, and weedy areas are also found in coves and around the islands in mid-lake.

Lake Iroquois is a nutrient rich lake, and thermal stratification is found only in the southern half of the lake in summer. Fish the weed beds in the northern section of the lake, and the coves and islands in spring, and the drop-offs and thermal layers of the southern half of the lake in summer. In the fall, the shallows are your best bet.

Smallmouth here grow heavy, and some nice specimens of several pounds or more have been taken here in recent years. The largemouth population is good, and some fair fishing for old mossyback can also be had. Pickerel weed beds can be trolled with a weedless rubber worm and will produce largemouth during the summer.

A fairly steep drop-off on the southeastern and western shoreline, where the area is hilly and wooded, will bring good smallmouth action during warmer weather, also.

Very few facilities for lodging, dining, and so forth are offered near the lake; it will require a 10- to 20-mile drive to find such services.

Lake Carmi

Lake Carmi, located in Franklin, close to the Canadian border, boasts an excellent smallmouth fishery in its 1,417 acres.

The lake is situated in rolling pasture and mixed hardwood and softwood groves. A dam, situated on a mill pond on the outlet of Lake Carmi and owned by the Vermont Department of Water Resources, is used to stabilize the water level, keeping the maximum depth of the lake at 33 feet.

Lake Carmi is a soft-water lake with a high population of plankton. The balance between fish populations is excellent, with the northern pike keeping yellow perch and pumpkinseed populations in check; this helps the smallmouth population remain stable.

During the summer months, oxygen is adequate only to the 25-foot level, so your fishing should be no deeper than that. Weedy areas at points all around the lake in shallower areas near shore are the best areas to fish in early spring.

Lake Carmi State Park, situated on the southeastern shore, offers 144 campsites, 35 lean-tos, showers for campers, and two boat launching areas, as well as swimming and picnicking.

Mill Pond Campground on Rte. 120, located on the pond at the outlet on the northeast end of the lake, is a private campground offering 45 large

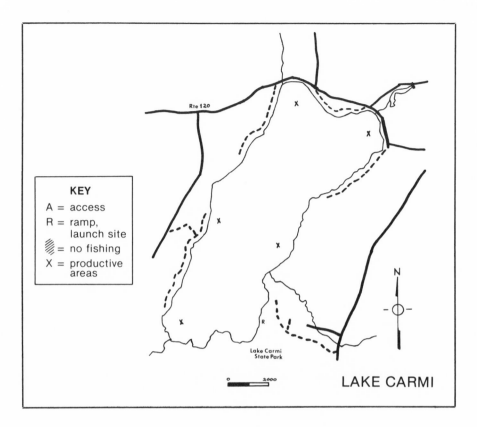

KEY

A = access
R = ramp, launch site
⬛ = no fishing
X = productive areas

Rte 120

N

LAKE CARMI

0   2,000

wooded and open sites, electric hook-ups, hot showers, and other facilities. It is open from June 18 through October 8 and weekends from May 18 to June 18. Call (802) 285-2240 for more information.

Lake Fairlee

Located in the Piedmont highland plateau lakes region of Vermont, Lake Fairlee is 427 acres of excellent largemouth and smallmouth fishery. The lake is moderately rich in nutrients and has good areas of vegetation and weeds. It has a maximum depth of 51 feet. A thermal layer during summer is usually found between 20 and 30 feet, and this is the level to fish during warmer weather.

Lake Fairlee was formed by the glaciers, and is actually situated in a kettle hole left by the ice mass. Route 113 actually passes through an ancient river valley between Lake Fairlee and the Connecticut River. The lake drains into the east branch of the Ompompanoosuc River; a small private dam controls the water level.

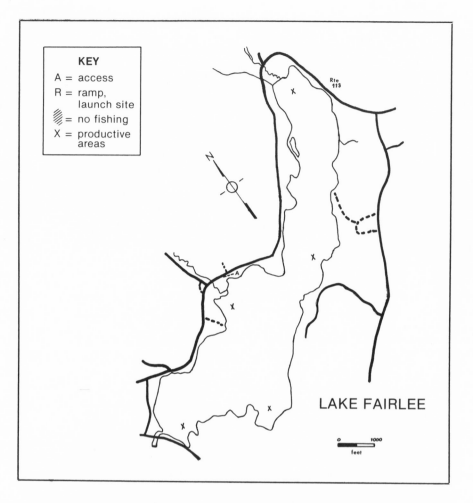

LAKE FAIRLEE

The mouths of Middle Brook, Blood Brook, and Mitchell Brook where they drain into the lake, are good areas to fish. The shoreline is mostly forested, with hardwoods and conifers, and there is some pasture land. The western and northern shores are moderately developed, with a number of youth camps in the area. Access to Lake Fairlee is located on the northern shore on Route 113.

The lake is noted for its bass fisheries and will offer many pleasant hours of fishing during your stay in Vermont. Thetford Hill State Forest, located close by, offers tent and trailer sites, as well as picnicking facilities.

The Rest N' Nest Campground on Latham Road out of Thetford Center (one-quarter mile from Exit 14 off I-91, east on 113 for 200 feet, then left at Commuter Park sign to Latham Road) offers 45 sites with electric, water, and all facilities. For more information call (802) 785-2997.

Lake St. Catherine

Route 30 passes to the east of another great Vermont bass lake, Lake St. Catherine. Located in the towns of Wells and Poultney, Lake St. Catherine occupies 910 acres of Rutland County. The maximum depth of the lake is 64 feet and large central expanses of the lake are deep swaths cut out of the lake bottom.

Both largemouth and smallmouth thrive here. During spring, largemouth can be found in a shallow weedy area in the northern part of the lake, called Lily Pond. Particularly interesting is an inlet stream to Lily Pond. The bass sit on the edges of its flow into the lake to feed.

The rockier mid-section on the western shoreline where the land juts out to a point and the water drops off rapidly to 23 feet is a great honey hole for bronzebacks. There are also a myriad of other spots like this to explore on Lake St. Catherine.

The Vermont Fish and Game Department maintains access to the lake on Route 30, and a private marina is located on the lake to supply you with any of your boating needs.

Lake St. Catherine State Park offers both wooded and open campsites, sandy beaches and fishing access. Write for more information: RFD, Poultney, 05764, or call (802) 287-9158 or 773-2733.

Lodging, dining, and other facilities are generously sprinkled throughout the area to help make your stay at Lake St. Catherine a pleasant one.

The Connecticut River

By far one of the best bass rivers in the northeast, the Connecticut River, shared by Vermont, New Hampshire, Massachusetts, and Connecticut winds from a narrow faster-flowing river to the north to a slower-paced wider bass heaven at the south. A 22-mile stretch between the dams above Massachusetts' Turners Falls to the Vernon Dam offers excellent bass fishing from late May through mid-June.

Rubber worms cast at the banks and in and around structure along its length produced some lunkers most any time we have fished there. The Vermont largemouth record of eight pounds was taken from the Connecticut in 1977.

Follow Route 5 and try: the area at Brattleboro at the junction of Route 9; the area south of Westminster; the area south of Bellows Falls; the area at the Wethersfield Bow; the portion of the river at Pompanoosuc, where the West Branch River connects with the Connecticut; and at South Newburg at Hollis and Peach brooks.

The Connecticut originally supplied, and still does in certain areas, most of the power for industry in the region, and many hydroelectric dams dot its length. It is important to be careful when exploring the river, and it pays to scout ahead or obtain a good map of the river before embarking.

Canoe access points are situated all along the river; generally, this is a good river to explore slowly in that fashion.

Bass tournaments are held every year on the river with good results; lodging, dining, and other facilities abound up and down its length.

Wilgus State Park is a small campground that is perfect for canoeists on the Connecticut, with lean-tos and tent sites located on the river bank. To contact them, write Box 196, Ascutney, Vt. 05030, or call (802) 674-5422 or 773-2657.

Some More Important Bass Waters in Vermont

ADDISON COUNTY

Lake Dunmore (Lake Dunmore): Route 53; a spring-fed lake, Dunmore has heavy traffic in the summer, but early morning and late evening finds few, if any, other boaters; crayfish, crayfish artificials and rubber worms fished at the lower end of the lake produce LMB; boat rentals and camping on the lake.

CHITTENDEN COUNTY

Arrowhead Mountain Lake (Georgia, Milton): 826 acres; 25 feet maximum; a long narrow lake formed by a dam on the Lamoille River, this lake is fed by over a dozen small brooks. Route 7 follows its western shore; SMB action is good here along the river creek bed and in and around the islands in the northeastern arm of the lake.

***Shelburne Pond** (Shelburne): out of Shelburne Falls, Vt. off Route 116; 449 acres; 25 feet maximum; SMB fishing in this lightly developed pond is great as the recent annual state record of 5 lbs., 10 ozs. taken in 1982 can illustrate; Shelburne Pond is nestled in rolling farmland and Fish and Game access to the pond is obtained off Route 116 on a dirt road, Pond Road; extensive weedy shallows surround the pond on the western, southern, and northern shore but the eastern shoreline drops off sharply.

FRANKLIN COUNTY

Fairfield Pond (Fairfield): out of St. Albans on Route 105; 472 acres; 42 feet maximum; SMB fishing along steep drop-offs, particularly on the eastern shore, is good; small area around islands on southwestern shore holds some good ones, too; boating access off town gravel road.

Metcalf Pond (Fletcher): out of Fletcher on unpaved town road; 81 acres; 25 feet maximum; good SMB fishing in the area surrounding islands at mid-lake on both eastern and western shores; this is the area where numerous drop-offs attract the bronzebacks; small boat access off dirt road.

LAMOILLE COUNTY

Lake Eden (Eden): Route 100; 198 acres; 40 feet maximum; SMB fishing excellent in several deep drop-offs in various areas along the lake; moderately developed with a Boy Scout camp located on the eastern arm of the lake; the Vermont Fish and Game Dept. maintains a boating access on Route 100 on the northeastern shore.

ORLEANS COUNTY

Little Hosmer Pond (Craftsbury): off Route 14 on Town Hwy. 7; 183 acres; 9 feet maximum; Little Hosmer is a shallower pond favored by LMB and like its larger connected neighbor, Big Hosmer Pond, which gave up a seven-pound LMB in 1981 for the annual record, Little Hosmer holds promise; extensive weedy areas fished with weedless rigged worms in early spring and fall can produce lunkers; Dept. of Water Resources provides access at the dam on Town Hwy.

RUTLAND COUNTY

*Sunset Lake (Benson): gravel Town Hwy. 43 off Route 73; 195 acres; 188 feet maximum; moderately developed with a Boy Scout camp located on the eastern shore; both LMB and SMB action is good here with drop-offs your best bet; trolling deep-runners in summer is a good action starter; boat launching at dam area off Town Hwy. 43.

*Glen Lake (Benson, Castleton, Fairhaven): off Moscow Road abutting Bomoseen State Park; 202 acres; 68 feet maximum; this lake is shadowed by the great Lake Bomoseen but offers excellent fishing for both LMB and SMB as well; the area around Obrien Point drops off nicely for summer fishing and in spring LMB can be found in the weedy shallow northern arm of the lake; access can be found through the state park.

*Sunrise Lake (Benson, Orwell): on gravel town road from Route 73; 76 acres; 43 feet maximum; moderately developed with a Boy Scout camp sandwiched between it and Sunset Lake off Sunrise Lake's western shore; both LMB and SMB fishing is good with LMB found in shallow northwestern arm of lake in spring.

*Lake Hortonia (Hortonia): Route 144; bass fishing at its best; the state record for LMB was broken here in 1982 with an 8 lb., 4 oz. lunker; both LMB and SMB populate the lake.

WASHINGTON COUNTY

Valley Lake (Woodbury): out of Woodbury off Route 14 on unpaved road; 73 acres; 70 feet maximum; rocky bottom; SMB fishing good especially along drop-offs and submerged rock on southeastern shoreline; deep hole in mid-section of lake good in warm weather; boat launching on unpaved road.

*Lake Greenwood (Woodbury): Route 14; 78 acres; 41 feet maximum; SMB thrive here and early spring fly-fishing in the shallows is a treat every fisherman should try; in summer drop-offs in southeastern arm around a large island are good places to try; Vermont Fish and Game maintained access is located on Route 14.

*Molly's Falls Reservoir (Cabot): Route 2; 411 acres; 35 feet maximum; Molly's Falls is a SMB heaven. The shoreline is covered with large rocks and boaters should beware of the many large boulders submerged around the reservoir. Fishing is good around Sand Island at mid-lake on eastern shore and along a rocky shallow area along southeastern shoreline where a large boulder called Mother Rock drops from 2 to 10 feet depth on one side. This is a dangerous area to fish unless you are fishing slowly and carefully; Vermont Fish and Game Dept. access is near the Marshfield Dam on Route 2.

WINDSOR COUNTY

A "mini" bass lakes region exists in Windsor County along Route 100 between Ludlow and Plymouth, Vermont. Six lakes, all part of the Black River System, are located within minutes of each other and offer superb bass fishing.

Reservoir Pond, Lake Rescue, Amherst Lake, and Lake Ninevah offer great LMB fishing and Echo Lake and Tiny Pond have good SMB fisheries. A stay in this area will offer a fishing trip with no end of possibilities to try — certainly not a boring area of the state for bassmen.

APPENDIX

For more information on licensing and regulations:

Dept. of Inland Fisheries and Wildlife
284 State St. - Station #41
Augusta, ME 04333

Division of Fisheries and Wildlife
Leverett Saltonstall Bldg.
Government Center
100 Cambridge St.
Boston, MA 02202

New Hampshire Fish and Game Dept.
Box 3003
34 Bridge St.
Concord, NH 03301

Department of Environmental Mgmt.
Division of Fish and Wildlife
Government Center, Tower Hill Rd.
Wakefield, RI 02879

Vermont Fish and Game Dept.
Montpelier, VT 05602

Division of Fisheries and Wildlife
Statehouse
Hartford, CT 06101

BASS CLUBS

Connecticut BASS Federation
10 Roger Ave.
Cheshire, CT 06410
(203) 272-9210

Maine BASS Federation
117 Country Club Rd.
Sanford, ME 04073
(207) 676-3188
(207) 324-2602

Massachusetts BASS Federation
10 Milford St.
Upton, MA 01568
(617) 529-3901

No matter which state you fish, New England has a lot to offer.

North Eastern BASS Association
P.O. Box 82
Indian Orchard, MA 01151
(413) 543-8051

Commonwealth Bassmasters
5 Sonoma Dr.
Worcester, MA 01602
(617) 852-4177

East Coast PRO-BASS
P.O. Box 123
Marlborough, MA 01752
(617) 485-4051

NH BASS Federation
12 Woodhaven Circle
Merrimack, NH 03054
(603) 424-9560

Boston Bass Anglers
13 Burch St.
Arlington, MA 02174
(617) 648-3546

RI PRO-BASS
66 Theresa St.
Woonsocket, RI 02895
(401) 766-5957

CT River Bassmasters
131 Vermont St.
Holyoke, MA 01040
(413) 532-3493

BOATING

The United States Power Squadron (USPS), originally a division of the Boston Yacht Club, became a separate entity in 1914. They offer a boating course in the spring and the fall and it is open to anyone 12 years and older. Enrollment is free. A good book to use for their course is Chapman's "Piloting, Seamanship, and Small Boat Handling".

The United States Coast Guard Auxiliary offers a Boating Skills and Seamanship Course, also. Check with your local Coast Guard office for more information.

Many local Red Cross Chapters offer boating safety courses, also.

For more information on Vermont and Lake Champlain:

Lake Champlain Regional Chamber of Commerce
209 Battery St., P.O. Box 453
Burlington, VT 05402

Vermont Department of Tourism and Development
Montpelier, VT 05602

Marine Division of VT Dept. of Public Safety
Montpelier, VT 05602
Write for free pamphlet "Laws and Regulations Governing the Use and Registration of Motorboats"

For more information on Rhode Island:

Greater Providence Convention and Visitors Bureau
10 Dorrance St.
Providence, RI 02903
(401) 274-1636

RI Tourist Promotion Division
(401) 277-2601
Toll free 1-800-556-2484 (Except RI)

Travelers Aid Society of RI
46 Aborn St.
Providence, RI
521-2255

For more information on State Recreation areas, including permits for the use of fireplaces contact:

Department of Environmental Management
Parks and Recreation Division
83 Park St.
Providence, RI 02903 or contact the individual park.

For more information on all areas of New England contact:

The New England Vacation Center
630 Fifth Avenue
New York, NY 10020
(212) 307-5780

For more information on the acid rain programs contact:

New England Interstate Water Pollution Control Commission
607 Boylston St.
Boston, MA 02116
(617) 437-1524